René Polette

Wonderful
LOIRE VALLEY
CASTLES

Photographs by: Hervé Champollion

Hervé Champollion is represented by TOP-RAPHO, Paris

Translated by: Angela Moyon

ÉDITIONS OUEST-FRANCE

13, rue du Breil, Rennes

Table of contents

Dear Reader

This guide is designed to make you want to visit a castle for the special features that make it what it is and, once you have finished your visit, to file it away in your memory like a key, ready to unlock a door sometime in the future. The descriptions are in five parts. **Outstanding Features** gives a brief description of the most outstanding points of interest. **History** describes the main events in the life of the castle, with facts and historical figures. **Tales and Anecdotes** contains a few amusing episodes that put flesh on the bones of History. **Architecture** draws your attention to the aesthetic beauty of certain essential parts of the exterior and interior. **Heritage** is designed to satisfy the cultural appeal felt by every one of us when faced with an old building and to answer the questions we ask ourselves when looking at furniture, a painting,

tableware, a sculpture, or a tapestry, whether we are drawn to them because of their beauty, or their historical and sociological value. A summary at the end of the book resumes the topics covered during the visit.

Before you set off to visit these buildings, may we remind you that the new generation of curators and owners sees the castle in their care as a living structure. In an attempt to meet the demands of a general public avidly seeking

Chambord.
South wall: the royal entrance.

knowledge and beauty, they organise appropriate cultural events (e.g. concerts, drama productions, lectures, seminars) and provide particularly attractive layouts (flower decorations, beautifully-displayed exhibits, visits-on-a-theme, and explanatory notes). By doing so, they create the links that help visitors to understand the very character of the building, without necessarily realising that they are doing so. This answers the fundamental questions that any visitor is bound to ask. What were the castle's origins? What was its purpose? What happened to it over the ages? What remains of the original? Was it subject to successive periods of destruction, extension and restoration? What use is it now? What can we learn from it? Why bother to stop, look, admire, fall in love with, and preserve it? All this forms the basis of a sustainable, profound interest because the deeper the love the greater the interest and vice versa.

Amboise

Foreground: Hurtault Tower, St. Hubert's Chapel. Louis XI towers. Middle ground: royal apartments. Right: the park and the site of the Collegiate Church of St. Florentin.

OUTSTANDING FEATURES

*History is present in every nook and cranny of this castle,
which marks the transition from the Gothic style (St. Hubert's
Chapel, Charles VIII Wing) to the Renaissance (Louis XII Wing).
The extensive collection of furniture and furnishings dates from
the Gothic, Renaissance, Empire, Restoration and Louis-Philippe
periods and is particularly attractive.*

A bracket on the Hurtault Tower.

Minims' Tower: intersecting ribs in the Chamber of States (Charles VIII Wing).

St. Hubert's Chapel: transept crossing (Flamboyant Gothic).

HISTORY

The feudal castle was confiscated in 1431 by Charles VII from the Viscount of Thouars who had been plotting against the monarch. Louis XI created the Order of Chivalry of St. Michael here, to counter the Order of the Golden Fleece set up at the rival Court of Burgundy. This was a major instrument of power linking great noblemen to the king himself. The sovereign settled Queen Charlotte of Savoy and her children in the castle and it was here that Charles VIII was born. Later, he was to express a wish to turn the castle into a palace more splendid than any other. He spent his married life with Anne of Brittany here, in true wedded bliss, and commissioned a number of major constructions such as the Charles VIII Wing and St. Hubert's Chapel. When he returned from Naples, where his Italian campaign had taken him, he brought back Italian artists and craftsmen who were the first people to spread the artistry of the Renaissance through France. The first Renaissance garden, for example, was laid in the castle grounds by a monk named Don Parcello. The king died after hitting his head on the lintel of a door (it no longer exists). Louis XII married the widow, Anne, in accordance with a clause in the first marriage contract which stipulated that the queen would marry Charles VIII's successor if he died without leaving a male heir. The newlyweds spent very little time in the castle although they made numerous improvements to it; instead, they preferred Blois. When the king died without a male heir, he was succeeded by his cousin, François I, who had been brought up in Amboise by his mother

*Slender columns decorated alternately with fleurs-de-lys and ermine tails
in the Chamber of the States General.*

St. Hubert's Chapel after the collegiate church had been destroyed (during the days of the Empire). In 1560, the town was rocked by the Conspiracy of Amboise fomented by the Huguenots. Its aim was to remove the young king, François II, elder son of Catherine de' Medici and Henri II, from the influence of the de Guise faction. The conspiracy was discovered and savagely punished. In fact, it was the first violent act in the Wars of Religion. Louis XIV only passed through Amboise on his return from Spain where he had married the Infanta, Maria Teresa. Intendant Fouquet and Lauzan were then imprisoned in the castle. Later, it became the property of the Duke de Choiseul, a government minister under Louis XV. During the Napoleonic Empire, four-fifths of the castle were destroyed by a greedy senator who sold off the building stone, a fate that befell many of the Loire Valley castles, churches and abbeys. During the Restoration of the monarchy, the grandiose ruins were given to the Duchess d'Orléans. Her son, King Louis-Philippe, and his grandson, the Duke d'Aumale, then launched a vast restoration project with the assistance of the architects from the *Monuments Historiques* (the French equivalent of the National Trust). Emir Abd El Kader was imprisoned in the castle from 1848 to 1852. Twenty-five members of his suite were buried in the park. The Emir was freed by the future Napoleon III.

Louise of Savoy, and who was married to Claude of France, daughter of Louis XII and Anne of Brittany. Although the royal couple were resident in Blois, they were frequent visitors to Amboise where they spent some considerable time, enjoying the luxury, entertainments and ceremonials organised by Leonardo da Vinci. He had come here from Italy in 1516 and he died (in 1519) at his home, Cloux Castle (now Le Clos-Lucé). He was buried in the chancel of the Collegiate Church of St. Florentin, within the castle, on the spot where visitors can now see his bust in the park. Later, his remains were moved to

Dormer window, Louis XII Wing.

Dormer window, Charles VIII Wing.

TALES AND ANECDOTES

The 3-year-old Margaret of Austria, daughter of Emperor Maximilian, was betrothed to Charles VIII, then aged 13, and she lived at the Court of Amboise. For political reasons, however, the young King married Duchess Anne of Brittany when he was 21 and she was 14. Anne, meanwhile, had been betrothed to Maximilian of Austria by proxy. After marrying Anne, Charles VIII sent Maximilian's daughter back to her home country and, at the same time, "stole" from the Emperor the girl he had wanted to marry. The Emperor was bitter. Anne and Charles VIII had a very happy marriage. In seven years, she gave him three sons and one daughter, all of whom died young. The only son of François I to survive, the future Henri II, husband of Catherine de' Medici and lover of Diane of Poitiers, was christened in the castle on 25th April 1518. Leonardo da Vinci is said to have been the first person to introduce fireworks into Court life, using them as part of the entertainment organised in the castle. It was from the wrought-iron railings outside the windows in the Chamber of States that some of the Huguenot conspirators were said to have been hung in 1560.

Royal apartments: Charles VIII Wing (left), Louis XII Wing (right) ending in the François I Wing.

ARCHITECTURE

It must be emphasised that the building we see today was not only a palace but also a military stronghold of historical importance in the same way as Chinon, Loches and Blois. This is obvious from the towers and ramparts. It was, though, here that the transition from late mediaeval to Renaissance style began in France and in Blois that the Renaissance style reached its height. The Charles VIII Wing is a fine example of Flamboyant Gothic architecture, as is St. Hubert's Chapel, an absolute gem carved like a piece of lacework in stone by Flemish craftsmen. Note the admirable carved lintel above the door, with the legend of St. Hubert depicted on

A capital in the Chamber of States.

the right-hand side and the story of St. Christopher to the left. The door itself is an equally fine piece of work, dating from the 15th Century. The Charles VIII Wing was built between 1494 and 1496 while the king was in Naples and it was completed after his return by Italian artists who brought with them

all their skill and know-how. This, then, is basically a Gothic building with ribbed ogival vaulting and ornate dormer windows topped with pinnacles. The royal apartments, however, have no ostensibly defensive purpose. They were built solely for comfort with wide windows and open balconies like the ones overlooking the Loire. The vast Chamber of the States General is as light as it is splendid, with slender columns alternately decorated with fleurs-de-lys, the King's emblem, and ermine tails, the emblem of Anne of Brittany. Louis XII added on a wing set at right angles to these apartments; it was completed during the reign of François I. By this time, the fashion had changed and the Renaissance style is evident in the treatment of the architectural features such as pilasters and lantern turrets reminiscent of Classical buildings. The ceilings were no longer vaulted. Note the Minims' Tower which is almost 40 metres high and 20 metres in diameter. Carts and horsemen from outside could ride up to the terraces above on a spiral ramp flanked by wide bays that let light flood in. The carved brackets supporting the vaulting are admirable for their satirical sharpness. The hollow central part of the building forms a ventilation shaft, a remarkable innovation in the 15th Century.

HERITAGE

The castle is fully furnished with Gothic furniture purchased by the Princes d'Orléans, all of it original and of very high quality. There are some superb pieces of furniture from the Renaissance, Empire, Restoration and Louis-Philippe periods. Fine dresser (16th Century) and two Italianate Renaissance tables with leaves. Chest made of walnut wood covered with gold leaf (early 16th Century) that once belonged to Catherine de' Medici. Superb Gothic pulpit used by the Cardinal of Amboise who married Charles VIII. Brazilian rose-wood piano signed Ehrard.

St. Hubert's Chapel: a 15th-century door with a carved lintel.

Cardinal d'Amboise' Gothic pulpit

Angers

Schist walls commissioned by St. Louis and 13th-century towers on the residence of the Dukes of Anjou. The top sections of the towers have been removed.

OUTSTANDING FEATURES

The massive military architecture of this fortress, which was built on the orders of the King, the future St. Louis, always comes as a surprise despite the fact that the tops of the towers were demolished in the 16th Century. The castle houses the largest narrative tapestry to have survived to the present time viz. the Apocalypse Tapestry, a prestigious piece of work commissioned by Louis I of Anjou, designed by the artist John of Bruges and probably finished in 1380. Despite its faded appearance, it still gives some idea of the richness of the original colours. Indeed, they were discovered on the back of the canvas in 1982 when the backing fabric was changed.

HISTORY

The he first major castle built by Fulk III Nerra (early 11th Century) was the main seat of the Dukes of Anjou and remained in the family until it was confiscated from King John of England (1206) by Philip Augustus. In its place, Louis IX, the future St. Louis, had a huge fortress built (1230-1240). It was the largest in the kingdom and the formidable remains that can be seen today give some idea of its original size when it was built to withstand a possible attack by the Dukes of Brittany. Later, the castle was given to the Dukes of Anjou in apanage and it became their palace in the days of Louis I (late 14th Century), Louis II and Yolande of Anjou, his wife (early 15th Century). Their son, the Good King René, patron of the arts in all their forms, gave lavish receptions there. Louis XI took the castle back from René and appointed his chancellor, Jean Bourré, Governor. During the Wars of Religion, the fortress regained its original, military purpose. Henri III ordered its demolition but the work was, fortunately, interrupted. Henri IV put an end to the violent warfare in western France by celebrating, in the castle, the engagement of the son he had had by Gabrielle d'Estrées. The young man was César Vendôme and he became betrothed to Françoise of Lorraine, the daughter of the Duke

The royal apartments and Flamboyant Gothic chapel.

de Mercoeur, commander-in-chief of the Leaguers. The castle retained its garrison and became a State prison. Among its most famous prisoners was Fouquet, Intendant of Finances.

A close-up of the vaulting.

TALES AND ANECDOTES

The future Charles VII was removed from the pernicious influence of the Court while still a boy. His father, Charles VI, suffered from recurrent bouts of insanity and his mother, Isabeau of Bavaria, was much more concerned with the King's brother, Louis d'Orléans. The heir to the throne therefore came to the Court of Yolande of Anjou, a strong-willed woman who married him to her daughter, the future Mary of France. Yolande was to retain great influence over Charles VII and he sent Joan of Arc to her Court.

Fan vaulting in the spiral staircase.

ARCHITECTURE

Millefleurs tapestry.

The castle is shaped like an irregular pentagon covering an area of 25,000 sq. metres, flanked by 17 towers set very close together. This was an innovatory system of defence in its day (early 13th Century). Louis XI ordered a 10-metre moat to be dug - and it is still visible today. It was never filled with water. Blocks of slate-bearing schist were used to build the towers, with decorative white stone string-courses. The towers were originally 40 metres high but the top sections were removed during the reign of Henri III. Inside, the early 15th-century St. Genevieve's Chapel was built to house the Cross of Anjou (it later became the Cross of Lorraine after René's marriage to Isabelle of Lorraine) that was depicted on a keystone. The wooden door dates from the 15th Century. Outside, there is a spiral staircase with a magnificent fan-vaulted roof like the one in Baugé Castle (15th Century). The barbican (1451) was restored in the 19th Century. The Count's Palace was refurbished in the 14th Century and has a 12th-century door with moulding.

HERITAGE

The *Apocalypse* Tapestry, the largest woven tapestry (14th Century) without a backing. Photographs give it back the dazzling, lush colours of the original. The tapestry is difficult to understand but is of vital importance in the history of the Middle Ages and of Art in general. It is part of the treasure of Angers Cathedral and, since 1950, it has been displayed in a room that was specially refurbished as an exhibition hall for this one item. The room is now scheduled for modernisation. The work was commissioned by Louis I of Anjou in 1375 from John of Bruges, the famous painter to King Charles V. He produced the models and sketches, which were painted before the tapestry was woven. The draping of the clothes suggesting a sense of movement is one of the stylistic qualities that characterise his miniatures. Other tapestries are housed in the royal apartments including the "Angels bearing the Instruments of Christ's Passion" (Flemish, 15th Century), in the chapel and in the Governor's Residence (15th, 16th and 17th Centuries).

The Apocalypse Tapestry commissioned in 1375 from John of Bruges.

The Apocalypse Tapestry:
the knights.

Azay-le-Rideau

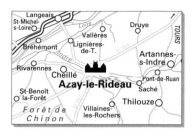

The castle reflected in the waters of the R. Indre.

OUTSTANDING FEATURES

How many poets and artists have celebrated the graceful beauty of this castle mirrored in the waters of the R. Indre? Yet visitors usually pay more attention to its interior than its exterior. This is unfair because the exterior is interesting for the symmetrical layout of the façades, and the ornate carved decoration on the monumental doorway. Also worthy of note are the flat, coffered ceilings decorated with medallions above the main staircase.

HISTORY

The estate of Azay was purchased by Martin Berthelot, Master of the Chamber of Accounts during the reign of Louis XI and Charles VIII (1465). His son, Gilles, was another of the kingdom's treasurers, thanks to his cousin, Baron de Semblançay, Governor General of Finances under François I. Gilles had the present castle built between 1518 and 1527, but his property was then repossessed by the king after the nobleman had fled to Metz following Semblançay's acts of embezzlement and subsequent execution. The castle was given to Antoine Raffin, one of the king's companions-in-arms at the Battle of Pavia who was then in captivity, like Jean le Breton. Later, the castle passed to the Béringhem and de Biencourt families, both of whom undertook major restoration work (19th Century).

Catherine de' Medici.

Virgin Mary with the Olive.

TALES AND ANECDOTES

The fortress that preceded the castle on this spot was overrun by the Burgundians. The future Charles VII was not permitted to enter it. He therefore took it by storm, hung the defending troops and burned down the village which then became known as Azay-le-Brûlé (Azay the Burned). François I, a great lover of castles, came to see the start of the rebuilding work in 1518.

Diana in her bath.

A huge entrance and the salamander, François I's emblem.

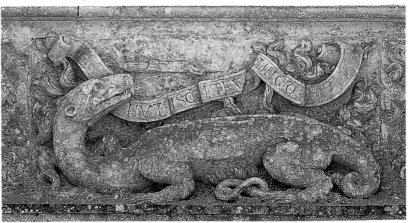

ARCHITECTURE

This building, commissioned by Gilles Berthelot, was one of the first Renaissance castles in France, which makes it historically and architecturally interesting even though it still contains mediaeval towers originally designed as a dissuasive feature, machicolations and even gun ports. In fact, this is a wonderful reconstruction in the Italianate style, using what remained of the half-demolished 15th-century castle. Built on an island in the Indre, it is traditionally admired for the reflections in the water that vary depending on the time of day. The R. Indre, though, was also chosen for its usefulness as a system of defence. The castle was built in an L-shape with a main section and a wing set at right angles to it, and is particularly interesting for its carvings and the layout of the façades. The huge entrance overlooking the courtyard and topped by a large dormer window is an attractive design in the Classical style that owes much to the influence of Italian architects. On the ground floor, there are four rows of semi-circular arches that are staggered compared to the windows on each side, with fluted pilasters on a pedestal leading up to an entablature with frieze topped by the emblems of François I and Claude of France, daughter of Anne of Brittany (the salamander and the ermine). On the sides, tall slender engaged columns inter-

The wall overlooking the courtyard: the monumental doorway and the large dormer window above the innovatory main staircase (c. 1518) with its straight flights of steps.

spersed with niches follow each other right up to the last arches. The dormer window is decorated with various vertical motifs in the Italian style including candelabras flanking two small pediments inscribed with the initials of the king and queen. The interior of the two-flight staircase (the same style as was to be used in Chenonceau but, in this instance, with loggias on the outside) has a remarkable coffered ceiling with Classical medallions and hanging keystones. This superb staircase gives a foretaste of the functional and aesthetic importance of staircases in France in later periods, from Blois to Versailles. The symmetrical layout of the façades overlooking the courtyard and garden is eye-catching for the majestic rigour of the rows of windows, their uniformity in the horizontal plane and the moulded string-courses that mark out the regular network which was to

become one of the main features of the French Renaissance style.

The huge doorway and the dormer window decorated with Italianate motifs. Candelabras flank two pediments bearing the ciphers of François I and Claude of France.

HERITAGE

Dining Room - Three superb tapestries in the Classical style, verdures with grotesques (Flanders, c. 1580).

Bedchamber, 1st Floor - Tapestries illustrating three episodes from *Jerusalem Liberated* based on sketches by Simon Venet (early 17th Century). Splendid barguerno, a Spanish cabinet with inlaid ivory motifs and gold leaf (late 16th Century).

Great Hall - Four Audenarde tapestries (Flanders, late 16th Century). Scenes from the story of Solomon including *The Judgement*. Strange, vividly-coloured borders full of human figures such as children playing and satyrs. Outstanding tapestry (*The Three Fates*, Brussels 1500). One of the figures

The coffered ceiling over the main staircase.

is holding the thread of life, the second is spinning it and the third figure is cutting it.

West Chamber - Very fine, if unusual, embroidered bedcover with colours that are still remarkably fresh. It was never completed when made in 1705 and still carries traces of pencil markings.

Magnificent tapestries (Beauvais, 17th Century) from the series entitled The Sovereign's House. Hunting scenes at Vincennes Castle and Versailles under construction.

Dining room.

A close-up of the embroidered bedcover.

A barguerno with ivory-incrusted motifs.

Beauregard

East façade: arcaded gallery in Italianate style.

OUTSTANDING FEATURES

The Portrait Gallery commissioned by Pauldrier,
Advisor to Louis XIII, depicts the kings and queens of France,
the most outstanding of the country's ministers of state, and famous people from the history of
France and the remainder of the world, from Philippe de Valois to Louis XIII. This is the only such
gallery of its kind in France. The Bell Cabinet is an outstanding example of the study of a
16th-century Humanist and friend of Ronsard the poet who surrounded himself with works of art.

HISTORY

The estate of Beauregard belonged to Jean Doulcet, financier to Louis XII who raised him to the peerage. Purchased by François I, it was then given to René, the Bastard of Savoie (1524). Jean du Thier bought it in 1545 and built the stately home we see today. Paul Ardier, financier to Henri III, Henri IV, and Louis XIII, purchased it in 1617 for his retirement. He began the Portrait Gallery and the work continued for three generations thereafter. The castle had several different owners, including Louis Thillier (1912) whose restoration project was continued by the Gosselin family who are still the owners today.

TALES AND ANECDOTES

The picture of Joan of Arc (1622) in the Portrait Gallery shows a sturdy young brunette who would be well capable of wearing a suit of armour. This is in total contradiction to the republican tradition that has grown up since that time.

Top: *The Portrait Gallery and the portrait of Louis XIII on horseback.*

The so-called "Bell Cabinet" (16th Century).

ARCHITECTURE

The Bell Cabinet (16th Century) is a superb little room with gilded oak wainscoting carved by Scibec de Carpi, cabinetmaker to François I at Fontainebleau. The coffered ceiling, also made of oak, is carved with sleigh bells, like the walls which have the du Thier family coat-of-arms in the centre. The South Gallery has a French-style ceiling decorated with medallions representing the poets of the Pléiade. The ceiling in the Portrait Gallery was painted by

A piece of furniture (1625) that is one of the finest creations of its day. There is another identical piece in the Louvre.

The Bell Cabinet: a close-up of a painting on wood attributed to Nicolo dell'Abate (16th Century) representing an allegory of sculpture.

Jean Mosnier (17th Century) and the floor is covered with a remarkable set of Delft tiles depicting an army on the march. The 16th-17th Century kitchens have a supporting pillar that goes through the centre of the table and a fireplace bearing the date "1567" and a motto.

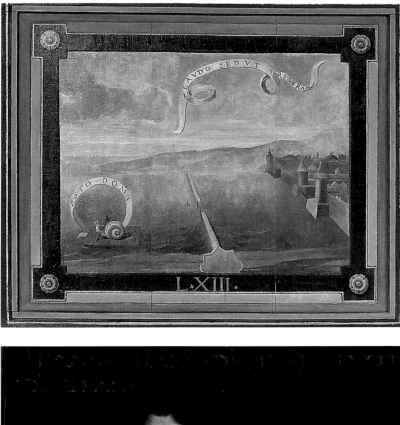

HERITAGE

Portrait Gallery - 327 portraits in 3 rows depict all the best-known people in the world, set out by reign over a period of three hundred years, beginning with Philip VI and ending with Louis XIII. The wall panelling was painted with allegorical scenes by Jean Mosnier (17th Century). One example is a dyke off La Rochelle and a raft carrying a snail that has been shot with an arrow. This was a snide allusion to the English who arrived too late to save their allies.

South Gallery - Outstanding piece of furniture (1625) whose "twin" is in the Louvre. Its panels were carved with mythological scenes, in the Renaissance style. Statue of St. Anne and the Virgin Mary carrying Jesus (wood, 17th Century). Also St. Michael slaying the dragon (alabaster high relief, 1511, Brandinelli).

Study known as the Bell Cabinet - Wainscoting decorated with superb 16th-century paintings, perhaps by Nicolo dell'Abate, representing man's favourite activities i.e. music, warfare, hunting, real tennis, sculpture, goldsmithing, reading, farming, and painting. See the superb, recently-created Marguerite Garden.

The dyke offshore from La Rochelle and the raft transporting a snail.

The Portrait Gallery.
A portrait of Joan of Arc which may be closer to the truth than the later republican tradition.

Blois

An aerial view of the castle.

OUTSTANDING FEATURES

This castle is a dazzling example of 16th-century royal magnificence and, as such, it is reminiscent of Chambord. Yet its "authenticity" is little more than a naive dream for, although it has retained a few traces of the developments and changes in its architecture, it is first and foremost an outstanding example of 19th-century restoration work. Indeed, it was taken as a reference for other such projects thanks to the genius of architect Félix Duban who achieved a masterly piece of architectural trickery by making the François I Wing an almost exaggerated example of the Early Renaissance style and the Louis XII Wing an almost excessive example of Late Gothic. The castle is also of major historic interest because of the important events that occurred there in the 16th and 17th Centuries.

Wonderful Loire Valley Castles

HISTORY

Central government established
itself on the west promontory before
the 10th Century. Guy de Châtillon,
the last Count of Blois, sold his castle
to Louis d'Orléans, the brother of King
Charles VI the Mad and husband of
Valentine Visconti, daughter of the
Duke of Milan. He was murdered by
John Lackland, Duke of Burgundy
and King of England (1407). His son,
Charles d'Orléans, a poet and highly
literate man, set up a library of fine
manuscripts in the castle. He married
Bonne d'Armagnac (1410) thereby
creating the Armagnac faction, arch
rivals of the Burgundians. He was
taken prisoner at Azincourt (1415) and
spent twenty-five years in England.
He then returned to Blois, married
Mary of Cleves (1440) by whom he
had a son, the future Louis XII.
Having been born in Blois (1462), the
monarch had his palace built on the
site when he mounted the throne
(1498). He launched a military campaign in Italy to lay claim to various
estates and was greatly attracted by a
country steeped in the Renaissance
style, from which he returned accompanied by architects and artists. He
extended the paternal library by
adding to it the works from Charles
VIII's library and the books he had
taken as booty in the Milan area, thereby creating the royal library of Blois
which, in 1544, was to join the royal
library of Fontainebleau. Together
they formed the basis of the National
Library. His wife, Anne of Brittany,
died in the castle. When the king died

The Loggia Façade overlooks the town.
It gets its name from the corbelled loggias flanked by pilasters.

*The François I Wing with its projecting spiral staircase opens onto
the exterior and was the first example in France of the
staircase-loggia with Italian-style balconies.*

without a male heir, he was succeeded by his cousin and son-in-law, François I (1515). François was strongly influenced by his mother, Louise of Savoy, whose emblem, two wings topped by a crown, can be seen in the François I Wing. The king had this wing added for Claude of France, daughter of Anne of Brittany and Louis XII, both of whom were very fond of the castle. He lost interest in the castle after his wife's death (1524) and transferred the seat of power to the Louvre which he had had refurbished. His sons and grandsons were to return from time to time to Blois, and a number of major historical events occurred there. During the Wars of Religion, for example, Catherine de' Medici, widow of Henri II who had been killed in a tournament, often came to the castle with her sons, each of whom was to be king in turn, in an attempt to bring Catholics and Protestants closer together amidst all the Court intrigue. It was in this context that Duke Henri de Guise was murdered during the States General (1588). He had been the leader of the Catholic League and had been plotting against Henri III. He died in the bedchamber of the monarch who was himself to die by the hand of an assassin, the monk Jacques Clément (2nd August 1589). This left the way clear for the dynastic pretentions of Henri de Bourbon, leader of the Huguenot faction and future King Henri IV. In the 17th Century, Marie de' Medici, the mother of Louis XIII, and Gaston d'Orléans, the king's brother, were successively exiled to the castle after taking part in conspiracies and intrigues.

The François I Wing. The dormer windows are decorated with candelabras and pinnacles flanking a niche with columns enclosing a figure carved in the Classical style.

The François I Wing: a column in the gallery with surbased arches. The diamond-shaped decoration encloses alternate fleurs-de-lys and ermine tails.

TALES AND ANECDOTES

The virtuous Anne of Brittany set up the Order of Grey Sisters to reward her equally wise ladies-in-waiting who were highly prized as wives by French and foreign noblemen. Claude of France launched the fashion for the plum that, in French, bears her name (the greengage, known in French as "Reine-Claude"). Catherine de' Medici wore mourning dress for Henri II for 30 years but it was black, in the Italian style, and not the royal white used in France. Because of this, she was known as the "Black Queen" and she died, in the castle, amidst general indifference, 12 days after the Duke de Guise.

Gaston d'Orléans Wing.

ARCHITECTURE

Louis XII had his royal apartments built between 1498 and 1501. All that remains of them today is the entrance wing and the start of the gallery in front of St. Calais' Chapel (now restored). The remainder was destroyed by Gaston d'Orléans. The wide windows, aligned vertically, bear witness to a new style of thought but Gothic taste is still evident in the grotesques above the windows and the dormer windows flanked by crocketed ogee arches. The flame-like decorations are characteristic of the Flamboyant Gothic style. Royal ciphers and emblems decorate the walls - the "L" and porcupine for Louis XII, the "A" and ermine for Anne of Brittany. The gallery with surbased arches like the ones in Talcy

Louis XII Wing. The dormer windows are flanked by crocketed ogee arches.

Top: *A porch in the Gaston d'Orléans Wing. The columns were never completed.*

has alternating columns and pillars. On the columns are diamonds decorated alternately with the fleur-de-lys that had been the emblem of the House of France since the days of Philip Augustus (13th Century) and ermine tails. Each pillar has an Italianate decor-

ation i.e. pilasters carved with a central vertical stem rising from a vase and bearing brackets, plant motifs and animals. This bucolic ornamentation, however, produces a sense of balance that was characteristic of the Renaissance and it can be seen again in the

François I Wing. A ceiling and fireplace in the reception room.

and horizontal pattern with the windows, doors and pilasters. The cornice on the top of the façade is ornately carved and is highly representative of the Italian style. Above it is a balustrade which partly conceals the dormer windows. The spiral staircase now has windows opening onto the outside; this was the first example in France of the staircase-loggia with Italianate balconies set between the buttresses to enable the Court to watch entertainment in the courtyard below. This type of staircase was to become commonplace and always had a decorative purpose. François I had a second building erected against the first one, on the other side of the original wall. He then connected them under the same roof (1515-1519). Opposite the town was the Apartment Façade with its corbelled balconies overlooking huge gardens containing Anne of Brittany's pavilion (now the tourist office) and the Orangery (now a hotel). Another floor had to be built above the balustrade with columns supporting the stretch of roof, so that rain water could drain off easily without spoiling the admirable symmetry and ethereal quality of the building as a whole.

The States General Chamber is one of the remains of the mediaeval castle, along with the Foix Tower, Dominicans' postern-gate and Châteaurenault Tower encased in the François I wing. The

François I Wing. This means that Italian artists were working for Louis XII as early as the end of the 15th Century.

The front of the François I building is even more richly decorated. To each side of the windows are pilasters topped by capitals. The dormer windows have pinnacles with candelabra flanking a columned niche containing a carving of a human figure in the Classical style. Each floor is separated from the next by a double horizontal string-course, creating a regular vertical chamber was used as a state room (13th Century) and is now the oldest Gothic vernacular building in France. It was restored in the 19th Century by Félix Duban who then included the great tierce-point bays opposite an extension added by Henri III but later destroyed. The impressive, magnificent oak rafters are original.

The Gaston d'Orléans Wing was suddenly abandoned after the birth of Louis XIV, as is obvious in a column devoid of fluting. However, the architect François Mansart, the uncle of the architect of Versailles, has given us a masterpiece of Classical Baroque architecture here, by including in the façade the architectural Orders common in Ancient Greece. Inside is the finest Baroque cupola in France. Its double oval is set within a quadrangle. The putti decoration (trophies, garlands of flowers) has never been finished. There is even a charcoal sketch. The staircase was added in 1932 and was a copy of the one in the castle in Maisons-Laffitte which had been designed by François Mansart. When, in order to erect the Gaston d'Orléans building, the 17th Century demolished a Louis XII wing, nobody expressed any remorse at the destruction of this piece of heritage. It was the Romantic Movement of the 1840's which rediscovered mediaeval and Renaissance architecture. One name stood out from the rest - Félix Duban (1797-1870). By res-

The tapestry of the Jeu de la Bascule *(16th Century). Louis XII Wing.*

toring Blois Castle, he was the first person to reappropriate a French Renaissance building. His work met with controversial reaction but people came from all over Europe, especially Britain (William Burgess, John Gregory Grace), to see the work and rediscover the Renaissance. Félix Duban based his restoration work on the remains of architectural features that could still be seen in the sculpture museum, on the remains of painted decorations, and on his personal research into old documents. His work restored the erstwhile glory of the castle and gave it the closest possible resemblance to its 16th-century appearance. To the castles of the Loire Valley, he gave an impetus that can still be felt to this day.

HERITAGE

The castle houses the Museum of Sculpture and Archaeology. The Art Gallery stands on the site of what were once Louis XII's apartments. There are so many treasures here that it is impossible to describe them all in detail. The pictorial works are particularly interesting, especially the ones by the Fontainebleau School. The extensive collection of French and Flemish tapestries from the 16th and 17th Centuries (some fifty of them in all) constitute a museum in their own right. One room contains a judicious collection of paintings dating from the New Empire period, all of them relating to the assassination of the Duke de Guise.

Brissac

The east wall with the huge round tower designed by Pierre de Brézé, counsellor to Louis XI.

OUTSTANDING FEATURES

The external architecture of this castle comes as something of a surprise. It is steeped in a strange, enchanting mediaeval power yet, at the same time, glorifies the grandeur of the reign of Louis XIV. The owners had been influential noblemen and courtiers since a member of the family had opened the gates of Paris to the future Henri IV. There is still a sense of majesty in this castle, where Louis XIII was reconciled with his mother. The furniture, all of it bearing the cabinetmaker's mark, is ornate and majestic. The castle also has decorated French-style ceilings, painted wainscoting, paintings, and tapestries (the most outstanding are the ones hung in the Hunting Chamber which date from the 16th Century).

The Chamber of Hunting.

The Louis XIII bedchamber.

HISTORY

A fortified castle belonged to the Counts of Anjou as far back as the 10th Century. Fulk III Nerra's grandsons, Fulk III le Réchin and Geoffrey III the Bearded each laid claim to it in order to gain ownership of the estate in Brissac. When the castle fell into the hands of a felonious nobleman, Philip Augustus had it razed to the ground. Pierre de Brézé, counsellor to Louis XI, rebuilt a fortress that once included the two large round towers still visible today. Louis de Brézé, Seneschal of Normandy, sold the castle before his marriage to Diane de Poitiers, the future mistress of King Henri II. The fortress purchased by René de Cossé (1502) withstood three sieges during the Wars of Religion, one of them led by Henri of Navarre. The fortress was seriously damaged and Charles II de Cossé-Brissac had it demolished and replaced by the castle we see today (1602-1621). It was here that the Queen, Marie de' Medici, was reconciled with her son, Louis XIII (August 1620) after the conflict opposing the two factions known as the "strange affair of the Ponts-de-Cé". The queen's confessor, the future Cardinal de Richelieu, organised the meeting. Successive Dukes of Brissac then resided mainly at Versailles, with the exception of Henri-Albert. He was a free-thinking rake and was exiled from the Court by Louis XIV.

TALES AND ANECDOTES

Charles I de Cossé-Brissac, an expert in ancient history, gave his son, Timoléon, a very intellectual education based on Latin and Greek. He was a brilliant young man but he unfortunately died at the age of 24, much to the despair of all who knew him. The poets of the Pléiade, Rémi Belleau and Jodelle, dedicated a collection of poems to him, "Tomb in memory of the death of Mr. Timoléon de Brissac". Also in his memory, all the male children of the family are given the Christian name Timoléon, as well as their own Christian name.

Charles II de Cossé-Brissac, Timoléon's younger brother, was a member of the Catholic League and Governor of Paris. He entered secret negotiations with Henri de Bourbon, pretender to the throne of France, prior to the latter's arrival in Paris. He succeeded in keeping at a distance the main Spanish military chiefs and their armies, posted loyal men in his own service at the gates of the city and had them opened during the night of 22nd March 1594. The people of Paris did not consider this act as treachery; instead, they made up a song which stated that, "Brissac saved Paris from damage ("bris") and pillaging ("sac")." Henri de Bourbon kept Charles II de Cossé-Brissac on as Governor of Paris and the post was handed down from father to son. In reward, Louis XII raised the Brissac estate to a duchy and its owners to the peerage (1620).

The grand drawing room.

The superb little theatre.

ARCHITECTURE

Two 15th-century machicolated towers flank the east wall consisting of three storeys of apartments and a tall domed pavilion. To the north is a wing set at right angles to the apartments, containing the guardroom and ending in the massive north-west pavilion which includes the bedchamber of Louis XIII. The south-east tower contains the chapel. The domed pavilion consists of four storeys with a semi-circular window flanked by niches on the first two floors and small semi-circular windows above. There is a different architectural Order for the ground floor and upper storeys, with rusticated pilasters in the style used for the Luxembourg Palace in Paris. The north-west pavilion is a seven-storey tower.

HERITAGE

The house contains exceptionally extensive collections of furniture, paintings, tapestries, and painted wainscoting. Note the outstanding tapestries (Enghien, 16th Century) in the Hunting Room said to have been given to the Count of Toulouse by Louis XIV and to have hung, at one time, in Rambouillet. The dining room includes a painting attributed to Pierre-Henri Martin. It shows *Bercy Castle*, on the site now occupied by the Gare de Lyon (railway station) in Paris. In the chapel (15th Century), there is a carved stall depicting David and *The parable of the mote and beam.* The tomb was carved by David d'Angers and decorated with sculptures by his father. There is an entire suite of furniture (18th Century) bearing the cabinetmaker's mark i.e. sofa, and six chairs covered with tapestry illustrating the Fables of La Fontaine. Portrait of the Duke de Maine, Louis XIV's son. Gallery of paintings. Superb Louis XIII staircase. Theatre laid out in the 19th Century.

The dining room with the painting depicting the Château de Bercy.

Chambord

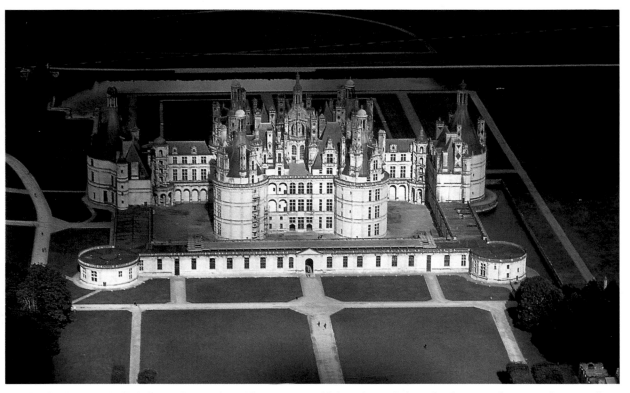

*Chambord was originally built as a fortress, but without a system of defence, hence the keep, four large round towers and outer wall.
To the left is the Dauphine Wing; to the right, the François I Wing.*

OUTSTANDING FEATURES

The prodigious exterior is a reminder of other extraordinary sights such
as the Temple of Angkor. This makes it one of the most famous historic monuments in the world
and it was included on the World Heritage list in 1983. The forest of towers, elegant bellcotes
and decorated chimneys, the cross-shaped rooms with coffered ceilings,
and its double spiral staircase constituted a prototype for the French Renaissance. Chambord is like
the pyramids in Egypt - it attracts researchers with never-ending questions, for much remains to be
discovered about this castle and mystery still shrouds its construction and its real purpose.

Wonderful Loire Valley Castles

HISTORY

Chambord is, first and foremost, François I, the last great French monarch of the mediaeval period, still influenced by the traditions of chivalry but also the first great French sovereign of modern times, determined to institute the concept of an absolute monarchy and who, through this building, wanted to display to the rest of Europe his majesty, and power. In this respect, he paved the way for the absolute monarchy of Louis XIV. The Louvre was the royal residence; Chambord was a showcase of royal prestige, and Charles V was received here amid great pomp and ceremony in 1539. The castle did not seem to have been built as a permanent place of residence. It was occupied for a mere twenty years over a period of almost five centuries and François I himself spent only forty-two days in it, to monitor progress on the building work, in a reign lasting thirty-two years. Chambord was the first of a long line of prestigious buildings such as Versailles, the Arc de Triomphe, and the Arche de la Défense. However, Louis XIV came here to hunt and, while here, he attended the first performance of Molière's *Monsieur de Pourceaugnac* and *The Progidious Snob* with music by Lully. The plays were performed on the first floor in the cross-shaped room above the entrance hall. In the 18th Century, the castle was the residence of the exiled King of Poland for

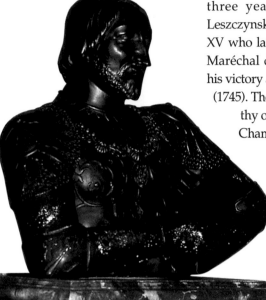

A bronze bust of François I.

three years. He was Stanislas Leszczynski, father-in-law of Louis XV who later gave the castle to the Maréchal de Saxe in gratitude for his victory at the Battle of Fontenoy (1745). The Maréchal led a life worthy of a royal here and died in Chambord in 1750, of wounds received during a duel. Nowadays, Chambord includes apartments in which the President of the Republic receives high-ranking guests invited to take part in presidential hunts.

The double-spiral staircase in the centre of the castle.

TALES AND ANECDOTES

The design of the castle is the subject of some controversy. Historians admit that François I requested a number of different projects from those around him and Dominique de Cortone left a model which closely resembles the castle. Leonardo de Vinci may have designed the central staircase. However, it would seem that the real designer and architect of this castle could have been François I himself, who picked out the innovatory ideas from each individual project submitted to him. The land was boggy and the building therefore had to be built on piles. They are made of oak and some of them are 39 ft. long, going down to a wide layer of hard rock. The piles are then interlinked to form a platform or base. The Count of Chambord authorised the use of his castle as a a field hospital by the Army of the Loire (1870) and, to provide heat for the wounded, the 17th and 18th-century wainscoting was used as firewood except for the panelling in the King's Bedchamber.

François I's study.

The keep as seen by Emperor Charles V of Spain during his visit in 1539.

Wonderful Loire Valley Castles

ARCHITECTURE

Exterior

Visitors approaching the castle from the car park are confronted by the dramatic majesty of the **rear façade** of Chambord, the view that is mostly commonly photographed. It is amazing to think that, in the 16th Century, this splendid, vast, and symmetrical building was already paving the way for the building of Versailles. Instead of rushing inside, take some time to stand opposite the royal entrance. From here, it is obvious that this is a 16th-century castle, built to the plans of a fortress. The central section is known as the **keep**, not because it served any military purpose with a system of defence but because the four huge towers at the corners give it a massive, mediaeval appearance as does the wall round about. It calls to mind ideas of chivalry, a concept to which François I, the Knight-King, was very attached. Indeed, it is known that the original plans (1519) consisted of only the keep. The traditional **parapet walkway** has been turned into a circular promenade decorated with modillions beneath the cornice. In the centre is the **lantern tower** that resembles a dome on a basilica church but it is topped here with a fleur-de-lys, the well-established symbol of the monarchy, rather than a Cross. To the right are the **royal apartments** eloquently decorated with fleurs-de-

The forest of chimneys and bellcotes with the lantern tower in the centre like a crown topped with a fleur-de-lys.

The dormer windows in the keep were enhanced with slate cladding in the form of geometrical motifs.

lys above the dormer windows and chimneys. François I died before the completion of this wing. To the left, set symmetrically opposite it, is the chapel which does not stand out from the remainder of the building as is the case in other castles but, instead, blends into the castle. The Cross was only placed on top of it in the 19th Century. In short, the external architecture was designed to emphasise the grandeur of the monarchy.

The **façade** clearly indicates the gallery (left) and windows (right), a layout which, according to the plans drawn up in 1519, was to be repeated on each side of the keep. This would have resul-

ted in a swastika shape as shown by the digs carried out on the foundations in 1994-1995. In 1526, however, it was decided to build the royal apartments to the right and to connect them to the keep by a wing. This in turn raised the question of access to the wing from the upper storeys in which

The King's Bedchamber.

The entrance to the keep seen from the courtyard.

Interior

In the keep, the empty space forms a **Greek cross** and the galleries or cross-shaped rooms are all of equal length. In the centre is the majestic spiral staircase. The use of this layout in Chambord was an innovation because until then it had been restricted to religious architecture, the finest example of it being St. Peter's Basilica in Rome (1506). The four cross-shaped rooms on the second floor have **coffered ceilings**. There are four hundred panels in all, two hundred of which are decorated with the salamander, François I's emblem. His motto was "I feed the good fire and extinguish the bad". One hundred and ninety-nine other panels bear the letter "F" topped by the imperial crown for the king claimed his right to be elected Emperor of the Holy Roman Empire; in the

end, it was Charles V of Spain who became Emperor. One of the panels in the room on the north side bears a capital **"F" presented as a mirror image**, a symbolic element that was found over and over again in property belonging to François I e.g. Fontainebleau, Saint Germain, and Villers-Cotterêts. This single mirror-image "F" is difficult to read for anybody standing underneath it. Above it is the terrace and the sky, a symbol of the divine presence. This means that the single "F" faced towards the one and only God, in a display of the one and only François I.

Each cross-shaped room has a doorway into each square apartment within each "arm" of the cross, and a fireplace. However, the doors are totally devoid of decoration and blend into the wall. There is a determined effort to highlight the view of the staircase in all its majesty, and to encourage people to use it.

Spiral staircases were a mediaeval tradition. It would have been a greater innovation to include a straight flight of steps in the Italian style, like the one in Chenonceau. Here, though, the staircase is a double spiral. This type of staircase had been used in Roman encampments where it facilitated the circulation of troops and had also been included in churches. This being so, it is not these two aspects that should attract our attention and that demand our admiration, even if they are often quoted. The extraordinary feature of this staircase is that it is treated like a building in

there were windows on this level. The windows were removed and replaced by a gallery on each floor. The windows were then repositioned on the rear wall in place of the galleries, which explains the admirable row of windows along the rear of the castle.

its own right, with a diameter of almost 30 ft, standing like a focal point on which the four cross-shaped rooms converge. It is completely traceried and it therefore acts as a backcloth for people using it. The hollow stairwell, with its twenty-four tiny windows, enabled people going up and down the staircase to see from one flight of steps to the other but, more importantly, they also enabled light to flood the staircase from outside. It stands right in the centre of the Greek cross, like the altar in a basilica church, but is not topped by a Cross. It is a fleur-de-lys that can be seen at the top of the lantern-tower above the staircase.

There are three **levels of apartments**, divided into four equal quarters by the Greek cross. The four corner towers have an apartment on the ground floor, level with the terrace, and one above. All the apartments are identical and are laid out symmetrically with a system of interior staircases. This was the first example of modular building in the history of France.

Bottom: *The coffered ceiling in the four rooms on the cross-shaped second storey.*

The central staircase: its hollow core containing tiny openings lets in the light from the lantern tower.

HERITAGE

The existing furniture and fireplaces were sold off in 1793. The royal suite has been refurnished as it was originally. It was the first apartment to be laid out in the French style, before Versailles was built. There are also reconstructions of apartments which were set out in 16th-century premises in the 18th Century. The ceilings, which originally stood 21 ft. above the floor, were lowered by hanging fabric below them and giving them a stucco finish. The François I apartments are still the original size but parts were partitioned off in the 17th Century and the decorative features have all disappeared. The castle houses a magnificent collection of tapestries, indeed it is one of the finest collections in the Loire Valley.

16th-century tapestries: *Abraham's Call* (Brussels, Sun Room, decorated with shutters ornamented with sun's rays, 17th Century). Series of tapestries illustrating the hunts organised for King François I (Paris) - *The Bear Hunt* (Tournai) - Series of tapestries illustrating the story of Diana the Huntress (Paris).

17th-century tapestries: Continuation of the story of Constantine (after Rubens, Paris) - Continuation of the story of Ulysses (after Simon Vouët, Amiens) - *Rape of the Sabine Women* (Flanders) - Continuation of the story of Meleager (Gobelins).

Note the collection of 18th-century French faïence, the carpets made in the Savonnerie works decorated with the French coat-of-arms (18th Century), the ceramic stove decorated with the coat-of-arms of the Maréchal de Saxe (18th Century), the gold-embroidered velvet hangings and bed (Italy 16th Century, François I Bedchamber), and the outstanding exhibits in the Hunting Museum (16th-19th century weapons including crossbows, arquebuses, guns, rifles, and pistols).

Chaumont

Diane de Poitiers was forced to move to Chaumont in 1560 in exchange when Catherine de' Medici took over Chenonceau after the death of Henry II (1559).

OUTSTANDING FEATURES

This majestic stately home is steeped in memories of outstanding destinies and serious setbacks, associated as it is with people such as Thomas Becket who was one of the castle's guests before he was murdered, Peter of Amboise and his children (all of them had brilliant futures in front of them), Diane de Poitiers who was sent here by Catherine de' Medici, Madame de Staël who was exiled to the castle by Napoleon, and Mary Say, a rich heiress whose life took her from the lap of luxury to absolute poverty. Among the outstanding contents of the castle is a superb series of tapestries (late 16th Century) on the theme of days and planets. Note also the outstanding majolica ware tiling (17th Century).

Wonderful Loire Valley Castles

HISTORY

The first castle, built in the 10th Century, was given to Gelduin by Count Eudes II of Blois to compensate him for the loss of his castle in Saumur (it had been taken from him by Fulk III Nerra). Through marriage, it passed to the family of Amboise for five centuries (1560) until Catherine de' Medici purchased it and gave it, a short time later, to Diane de Poitiers in exchange for Chenonceau. Before then, however, Pierre d'Amboise and his son, Charles I, had built the west wing we see today (1473-1481) and the north wing that was destroyed in the 18th Century. The estate then had various owners including Viscount de Turenne, the father of the famous Maréchal, and the d'Aramon and de Broglie families who restored it. Finally, in 1938, it became State property.

The courtyard looks out over the Loire. The north wing was demolished in the 18th Century. To the right is the west wing.

Majolica tiling (17th Century) made in Valencia (Spain).

TALES AND ANECDOTES

It was here that Henry II Plantagenet had his last meeting with Thomas à Becket before the archbishop's murder in Canterbury Cathedral. Pierre d'Amboise (15th Century) had 17 children including Louis who was Bishop of Albi and negotiated the return of Burgundy to France (1477), Jacques, Abbot of Cluny, who commissioned the building of the Cluny Residence in Paris, and Georges, who was a cardinal and had the first Renaissance castle built in Gaillon in Normandy. Jean-Donatien Le Ray, the castle owner in 1750 and a wealthy ship owner from Nantes, set up a pottery in the outhouses and induced the Italian engraver, Giovanni Battista Nini, to come and work there. He produced some remarkable medallions of famous men of his day including Voltaire, and Benjamin Franklin who was a frequent visitor to the castle. His son, a merchant in the U.S.A., opened the doors of his home to Mme de Staël after she had expressed her opposition to Napoleon. She held a salon here. Mary Say, the last owner (1875), was a wealthy heiress and the wife of Prince de Broglie. She gave lavish receptions for royalty and restored the castle. She died, almost penniless and totally forgotten, in Paris.

ARCHITECTURE

The surviving sections of Pierre d'Amboise' castle are all of the defensive type. There is the west wing with its rectangular tower, the keep also known as the Amboise Tower, and the perpendicular wing that is higher than the others and includes a parapet walkway and machicolations. Charles II, Grand Master of the royal household during the reign of Louis XII, built the entrance over the drawbridge, bearing his coat-of-arms. The arms on the tower to the right are those of Georges, the cardinal;

The fireplace in the dining room.

The majestic entrance on the south side with its two large towers carved with decorative features and its machicolated parapet walks.

The east wing and its carved balcony. The south wing has arches and an octagonal tower skirting a spiral staircase (late 15th Century).

HERITAGE

Library - medallions by Giovanni Battista Nini. Tapestries depicting Alexander in Babylon and Alexander in the presence of Darius, made to sketches by Le Brun (Aubusson, 17th Century).

Council Chamber - A complete series of 7 outstanding tapestries, each focusing on a god or a planet recalling the days of the week (Brussels, late 16th Century; they bear the mark of tapestry-maker Martin Reymbouts). Superb majolica tiling (17th Century) made in Valencia (Spain) and depicting a hunting scene. The glass windows include storied panes.

Prince de Broglie's stables (19th Century) - The most lavish stables of their day.

to the left are the arms of France and the monograms of Louis XII and Anne of Brittany. The East Wing overlooking the courtyard was restored by Paul Ernest Sauson (19th Century). It includes a carved balcony and windows with carved gables (16th Century) showing the arms of Charles I. The South Wing has arcades (18th Century) and is adjacent to a remarkable octagonal staircase tower (late 15th Century) that was a forerunner of what was to come in Blois and Chenonceau.

The majolica tiles and the Planets Tapestry (Brussels, 16th Century) in the Council Chamber.

Going up the inner staircase.

Chenonceau

An architectural gem straddling the R. Cher. In the foreground is Diane de Poitiers' garden; in the background, the Marks Tower and Catherine de' Medici's garden.

OUTSTANDING FEATURES

*This delightful horseshoe-shaped castle stretching from one bank of the River Cher
to the other is a gem of Renaissance architecture inside and out because of its ornate decoration.
It houses a number of outstanding decorative works. The castle was a love-nest, the home
of various famous women in history and the setting for lavish festivities.
Diane de Poitiers had a passionate love affair with Henri II here. Catherine de' Medici had
the two-storey gallery built in the castle in the midst of all the feasting and entertainment,
and Louise of Lorraine spent her period of mourning here after Henri III was assassinated.*

Wonderful Loire Valley Castles

HISTORY

Thomas Bohier, François I's Superintendent of Finances for the Milan area, had a delightful castle built in Chenonceau (1513-1517). It was his wife, Catherine Briçonnet, who monitored progress on the building work. Their son, Antoine, inherited the castle on the death of his father in Italy (1524) and his mother (1526), but François I took possession of it after Semblançay had gone to the block, claiming that his family had committed embezzlement. Once the castle was Crown property, it became a luxurious hunting lodge and received regular visits from "the Small Gang" i.e. François I, his mistress the Duchess

North wall. Italianate decoration with a balustered frieze.

of Etampes, the future Henri II, his mistress Diane de Poitiers and his wife, Catherine de' Medici. When François I died in 1547, Henri II gave the property to Diane de Poitiers who had a bridge built across the R. Cher behind the castle. After Henri II met his untimely death in a tournament, Catherine de' Medici took the castle back from Diane and gave her Chaumont in exchange. Catherine had a two-storey gallery built over the bridge and used it for lavish Court receptions during visits of her sons, each of them successive Kings of France. When she died in 1588, she bequeathed the castle to Louise de Vaudémont, the wife of Henri III. After the sovereign's assassination (1589), Louise retired to the castle for the period of mourning, during which she dressed in the royal white that was the usual colour of mourning at the French Court, hence the nickname of "White Lady". The castle was purchased by the wealthy Farmer General Claude Dupin (1733). His wife's secretary was none other than J.J. Rousseau and she received visits from philosophers such as Montesquieu and Voltaire. She was much loved by the villagers and, thanks to her, the castle escaped the damage that befell so many others during the French Revolution. In 1864, it was purchased by Mme Pelouze who had it meticulously restored until it regained as closely as possible the appearance it had had in the 16th Century. It has belonged to the Menier family since 1913.

The two tiers of galleries, each 60 metres - 195 ft. long, across the R. Cher.

A fireplace by Jean Goujon.

The ceiling in Catherine de' Medici's Green Study.

A portrait of Louis XIV by Rigaud, a gift from the monarch himself.

The interior staircase with its barrel vaulting, keystones and Classical coffering.

TALES AND ANECDOTES

Henri II was madly in love with Diane de Poitiers and he showered her with gifts, including some of the revenue from taxes paid on the country's bells. This led Rabelais to write that "The King has hung all the bells of the kingdom round the neck of his mare". The ladies-in-waiting to Anne of Brittany, when the Court was in Blois, were famous for their virtue; those who served Catherine de' Medici, on the other hand, were often forced to use their charms as a reward or as an argument in negotiations. Among the many lavish entertainments given in the castle, Catherine de' Medici had a naval battle acted out on the R. Cher (16th Century) in honour of her son, Charles IX. In the 19th Century, during a visit by President Jules Grévy, Mme Pelouze gave a Venetian evening with gondolas.

ARCHITECTURE

The Marks Tower was the keep in the original fortified pavilion. Built on the right-hand side, it counterbalances the protruding chapel to the left of the façade. The square apartments flanked by four turrets are built over the huge arches of an old mill inside which are the superb kitchens. The north wall overlooks the entrance and was restored in the 19th Century. It shows perfect symmetry in the layout of its doors and windows and in the design of the various

The Great Gallery which was turned into a hospital by Gaston Menier during the First World War.

45

sections and features of its roof. The decorative elements are Italianate as regards the pilasters flanking the bays, the double moulding with medallions between the storeys, the balustraded frieze running along the top of the façade and the large dormer windows resembling the ones in Blois.

The inner staircase was an innovation in its day and is quite outstanding. It has two straight flights of steps roofed with barrel vaulting and Classical coffering and leads up to a balustraded spiral section that lets light into the staircase as a whole. This section overlooks the Cher and has ogival vaulting.

A piece of furniture (16th Century) inlaid with mother-of-pearl and ivory and decorated with pen-and-ink drawings.

The Madonna and Child,
attributed to Murillo.

HERITAGE

The Child Jesus and St. John, *by Rubens.*

Guardroom - Tapestries illustrating scenes from castle life (Flanders, 16th Century). Remains of 19th-century majolica tiling.

Diane's Bedchamber - Two tapestries (*The Triumph of Charity* and *The Triumph of Force* - Flanders, 16th Century). Superb fireplace carved by Jean Goujon (16th Century). Painting of the *Madonna and Child* attributed to Murillo.

Catherine de' Medici's Study - Outstanding 16th-century ceiling. Painting: *Silenus in a Drunken Stupour* by Jordaens. Peacock tapestry.

Study - Painting of the *Holy Family* by Andreo del Sarto. *A Martyr* by Correggio.

François I Room - Priceless item of 16th-century furniture with mother-of-pearl and ivory inlay decorated with pen-and-ink

drawings. Painting: *The Three Graces* by Van Loo. *Diane de Poitiers* by Primaticcio.

Louis XIV drawing room - Portrait of Louis XIV by Rigaud in an outstanding frame that was a gift from the monarch himself. *The Child Jesus and St. John* by Rubens. *Mme Dupin* by Nattier.

First Floor Hallway - Series of tapestries (hunting scenes, Audenarde, 17th Century).

Cheverny

Built in the Louis XIII style, this is an outstanding example of 17th-century Classicism with symmetry as the main feature in its five pavilions.

OUTSTANDING FEATURES

*This is one of the most outstanding castles in the Loire Valley
because of its original furniture spanning the period from the reign of Louis XIV
to the days of the Napoleonic Empire. The fresh, vivid colours of its collection of tapestries,
the scenes painted on the wainscoting in the dining room,
the coffered ceiling in the King's Bedchamber and the grand staircase make this
a luxurious stately home which is of particular interest.*

HISTORY

Henri Hureau, Governor of Blois and Count of Cheverny, was the son of Philippe Hureau, Chancellor to Henri IV. It was Henri who had the castle built from 1625 to 1634. It has continued to belong to the same family except for one 70-year period, because it was sold by the family before the French Revolution and bought back once the situation had returned to normal. This, then, is a family home built to be lived in, and it still has its original decoration and furniture. The records do not mention any visits from historically famous people except the Duke d'Orléans' daughter, the Grande Demoiselle.

TALES AND ANECDOTES

Élisabeth, Henri Hureau's daughter, became Marquise de Montglas and organised lavish receptions attended by her friend, the Grande Demoiselle, who called the house the "Enchanted Palace". The 18th-century Orangery in the Classical style was used to store works of art that belonged to the nation (including Mona Lisa) from 1942 to 1944.

The west wall and the niches filled with busts of the twelve Roman emperors.

The Grand Drawing Room:
A portrait of Marie Johanne de la Carre Saumery, Countess of Cheverny, *by Mignard.*

ARCHITECTURE

This is a Louis XIII-style castle and an outstanding example of 17th-century Classical architecture. Its predominant feature is its symmetry. The windows are laid out regularly from bottom to top with a row of arched pediments and two rows of pediments with swirls facing each other. There is symmetry in the rounded niches containing the busts of twelve Roman emperors. There is symmetry in the alternating rectangular and semi-circular dormer windows. There is general symmetry in the apartments extending into a pavilion that rises above the level of the central section opposite the huge pyramid-shaped staircase. The French-style roofs on the main apartments and quadrangular domes topped by a lantern turret on the pavilions are also symmetrical. The façade is built of soft white stone; the rear of hard, rusticated stone. This was an innovation when the castle was built but it was to be used over and over again in later years. Inside, the dining room was shortened when a gallery was built in the 19th Century. The beams and joists were painted by Jean Mosnier, who depicted a few amusing episodes from the life of Don Quixote on the wood panelling (early 17th Century). The superb coffered ceiling (17th Century) in the King's Bedchamber was painted on the ground by Jean Mosnier then assembled in the Italian manner. It shows the story of Perseus and Andromeda. Unlike older spiral staircases, the great balustraded staircase has straight flights of steps and landings. It has been ornately carved with a profusion of garlands, coats-of-arms in a frieze, fruit and symbols of the Arts.

A close-up of the ceiling in the King's bedchamber.

The Grand Drawing Room.

Henri IV's travelling chest covered with Cordoba leather and stamped with the arms of France and Navarre.

HERITAGE

This is a stately home in superb condition, with a wide-ranging collection of furniture which has always been beautifully maintained. It dates from the Louis XIV, Louis XV, Louis XVI, French Regency and Empire periods.

Guardroom - Superb Gobelins tapestry (17th Century) depicting *The Kidnapping of Helen*. French Regency armchairs by Boulard. Henri IV's travelling chest covered in Cordoba leather and decorated with the arms of France and Navarre.

King's Bedchamber - Complete collection of six tapestries with ornate borders, woven to designs by Simon Vouet depicting the Labours of Hercules. They were made in the Paris workshops that were the precursors of the Gobelins factory. Louis XIV chairs covered in Aubusson tapestry.

Antechamber - *The Return of the Fishermen*, a remarkable tapestry after Teniers (Flanders, 17th Century).

Grand Drawing Room - *Joan of Aragon* (Raphael's studio). *Cosimo de' Medici* as a Young Man (attributed to Titian). Above the fireplace, the painting of the *Countess de Cheverny* is by Mignard. The writing desk was made by Stockel, cabinetmaker to Marie-Antoinette.

Vestibule - Three famous portraits by Clouet (16th Century) - Chancellor Philippe Hurault, his wife Anne de Thou, and Jacques Hurault, Philippe's brother. Three portraits by Rigaud (1659-1743) including one self-portrait.

Tapestry Chamber - Superb tapestries after Teniers (Flanders, 17th Century) depicting village games. Rare Louis XV Chinese-lacquered chest of drawers. Louis XV regulator in full working order decorated with bronze by Caffieri. It shows the time, date, day and phases of the moon.

A tapestry after Teniers (Flanders, 17th Century). Village Games.

A tapestry after Teniers (Flanders, 17th Century). The Return of the Fishermen.

Chinon

Left to right: Coudray Fort with the Mill Tower and the Boissy Tower used as a lookout post.
The middle castle with the royal apartments, Charles VII reception room and, on the right, the Clock Tower.

OUTSTANDING FEATURES

This formidable romantic ruin consists of
three fortresses in a single castle spread
out high above the town and the R. Vienne.
It was here that Joan of Arc met the heir to the throne,
Charles VII, in very special circumstances that made it the most famous meeting
in French history, and it was from here that she set out on the epic travels
which were to take her to Rheims where she crowned the King.

Wonderful Loire Valley Castles

HISTORY

This castle had a quite exceptional history. It was the main residence of the Kings of England from 1154 to 1205 then became the main residence of the Kings of France from 1417 to 1450. The first permanent castle was built on the plateau by Thibault the Cheat (10th Century), one of the Counts of Blois who retained ownership of the property until 1044 when Thibault III was forced to give it to Geoffroy Martel, Count of Anjou. In 1154, Henry II Plantagenet, Count of Anjou, became King of England. He had St. George's Fort built and extended the castle, where he lived and died in 1189. His elder son, Richard the Lionheart, was brought back to the castle in 1199 after being fatally wounded at the siege of Chalus-en-Limousin and was later buried beside his father and his mother, Eleanor of Aquitaine, in Fontevraud Abbey. His brother, John, married Isabelle of Angoulême there but then had his lands in France seized by the Court in Paris after he had murdered his nephew, Arthur of Brittany, Richard the Lionheart's son, in an attempt to steal the crown from him. As a result, he acquired the nickname John Lackland. The castle was attacked by Philip Augustus after a siege lasting one year (1204-1205) and became French Crown property. In the period before the future St. Louis came of age, Blanche of Castile gathered an army there to put down a revolt by leading noblemen. Philip the Fair held Jacques de Molay, Grand Master of the Order of the Temple, prisoner in the castle in 1308, along with other dignitaries of the Order. The future Charles VII, the "Little King of Bourges", who opposed Henry VI of England, "King of Paris", com-

Entrance to the middle castle is by way of the Clock Tower on the other side of a deep moat.

pleted the construction of the royal apartments and received Joan of Arc in the main State chamber, surrounded by his courtiers, on 9th March 1429. During Charles VII's reign, the king often returned to the castle with Agnès Sorel. She was the first official mistress of a king of France. During Louis XI's reign, the castle was governed by a chronicler named Philippe de Commines. Louis XII came here to receive Caesar Borgia, the papal legate who brought him the Bull cancelling his marriage to Jeanne, Louis XI's daughter. This enabled him to marry Anne of Brittany, widow of Charles VII. In 1634,

Cardinal de Richelieu became the castle's owner. In 1699, his great-nephew, Duke de Richelieu ordered the demolition of the State chamber where the famous meeting had taken place because the building as a whole was threatening to collapse. The castle was left to withstand the onslaught of time (and human greed) from 1631 onwards. Complete demolition was avoided thanks to Prosper Mérimée and work gradually began to shore up and save this grandiose ruin that had had such a prominent place in French history. The work is continuing at the present time.

Tapestry (Aubusson, 17th Century).
The Heir to the Throne is recognised by Joan of Arc.

TALES AND ANECDOTES

It is said that anybody who captured Marie-Javelle (the great bell) would regret it. And it has to be said that she successfully survived the Wars of Religion, the French Revolution and the Napoleonic Empire without anybody touching her. It was known that Agnès Sorel lived in the Reberdeau Residence outside the north wall of the castle where she had been installed by Charles VII himself in 1444. Legend had it that the king used to join her every night using an underground passage that has since been rediscovered, by chance, by a gravedigger. The passage does indeed lead to the site of the residence and its entrance is still visible in the dry moat between the middle fortress and the Coudray Fort.

ARCHITECTURE

The castle consists of three forts - St. George's to the east, the middle fortress beyond the Clock Tower on the other side of a deep moat; and Le Coudray to the west which is separated from the middle fortress by a moat. The Clock Tower (13th - 14th Centuries), which is preceded by a stone bridge and topped with machicolations, contains Marie-Javelle, the famous bell with the silvery tones produced by the addition of silver to the bronze of the bell itself, which has been ringing out the hours for the people of Chinon since

1399. This means that Joan of Arc must have heard it strike. The tower also contains the Joan of Arc Museum containing items found during archaeological digs, documents, reproductions, illustrated panels, and audio commentaries that are of great historical interest. The fireplace in the Throne Room, which is halfway up the wall, serves as a reminder of the day when Joan of Arc picked out Charles VII from among his courtiers. It was one of the great moments in the One Hundred Years' War and in the history of France. Also worthy of note are the Treasure Tower (13th Century), and the royal apartments (14th -15th Centuries) which have been partially restored and now house items that can be classified as "heritage". The polygonal Boisy Tower (13th Century) is topped with machicolations. On the upper storey, the ribs of the vaulted ceiling are supported on slender, carved lamp brackets. The Mill Tower stands at the south-west end of the castle and has ribbed vaulting springing out from a rose window (12th Century). The Coudray Tower (13th Century) stands 25 metres high. One floor has been demolished. Its walls are 3.95 metres thick. The tower was used as a prison for dignitaries of the Order of Knights Templar (1308) who left graffiti engraved in the stone. They can still be seen today (Cross and instruments of Christ's Passion, a profile of the Blessed Virgin Mary and the inscription J. Molay). Joan of Arc stayed in the tower when she came to Chinon. Georges de la Trémoïlle, a mere tool in the hands of Charles VII, was kidnapped one night by enemies who entered by a postern gate that can still be seen next to the Mill Tower. The Argenton Tower (15th Century) on the north side was a prison in the 17th Century and its walls are still engraved with graffiti (1631). There is also the Latrine Tower, and the Dogs' Tower (13th Century) which may have housed the royal hounds. It, too, has a room with latrines in it. The cylindrical tower is the 12th-century Lookout Tower.

A polychrome statue of St. Martin (15th Century).

HERITAGE

17th-century Aubusson tapestry depicting *Joan of Arc recognising the heir to the throne*. The figures are clothed in Classical dress. Polychrome statue of St. Martin (15th Century) who died in Candes not far away. Archaeology Museum.

La Ferté-Saint-Aubin

The castle is beautifully symmetrical.

OUTSTANDING FEATURES

*The lower section of this castle is built of stone from Apremont
in the département of Allier; the upper sections of the wall consist of brick made and fired on site.
It has the finest stables in the Loire Valley and its symmetrical architecture
gives the castle a quality that is characteristic of the 17th Century.*

Wonderful Loire Valley Castles

HISTORY

The building we see today was erected in the 17th Century for Henri de Saint Nectaire and the project continued under the leadership of his son, the Duke de la Ferté, Maréchal of France and companion-in-arms of Condé at the Battle of Rocroi. The work was interrupted when he ran out of funds. The Maréchal de Lowendal purchased the castle (18th Century). The Prince de Masséna, son of Napoleon's Maréchal, purchased it in 1816 and had the park relaid in the English style.

A terracotta horse's head (17th Century).

ARCHITECTURE

The architecture of this castle is of a very high quality. Its main feature is the use of brick, a traditional building material in this region.

TALES AND ANECDOTES

This residence was known as the "Marshals' Castle". It belonged successively to the Duke de la Ferté, Maréchal in the 17th Century, and to Maréchal de Lowental during the reign of Louis XV. Lowental purchased it when his friend, the Maréchal de Saxe, George Sand's grandfather, was unable to do so because of lack of funds. However, a few months later, the Maréchal de Saxe won the Battle of Fontenoy and the king gave him Chambord. The sovereign also paid for the castle's upkeep and the staff. The two marshals were then neighbours and they had a road built along the banks of the River Cosson so that they could pay visits to each other easily.

The dining room.

Indeed, the castle had its own brick-works in the 17th Century. The symmetry and regular layout that were characteristic of the century are apparent from the porch. They are obvious in the main apartments where verticality predominates thanks to the tall pilasters rising to brackets flanking the windows. On the first floor, the windows are topped by triangular pediments. Each vertical span rises to a tall dormer window with Mannerist friezes and ribbed arches supporting a firepot in the centre. This was a hallmark of all the great stately homes of the 17th Century such as Villandry. The stables flanking the courtyard, one set of which is small and the other large in accordance with the fashion set in Versailles, have superb interiors now that restoration work has been completed. The exteriors (17th Century) are equally fine with terracotta horses' heads reflecting the luxurious lifestyle of the Maréchal de la Ferté, Governor of Lorraine and an enthusiastic huntsman.

A portrait of Louis XV at the age of 54. This was a gift from the king himself.

HERITAGE

Guardroom - Wonderful 17th-century French ceiling decorated with the coat-of-arms of the Maréchal de la Ferté. Tapestries include a verdure (Lille, 18th Century) and an illustration of an episode in the Thirty Years' War (Aubusson, 17th Century).

State drawing room - Louis XVI chairs. 18th-century Murano glass chandelier. Unusual portrait of Louis XV at the age of 54, a gift to the Maréchal de Lowendal from the king himself (Maupetit studio).

Fougères-sur-Bièvre

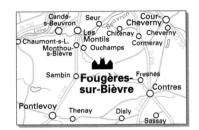

A late 15th-century fortress.

OUTSTANDING FEATURES

*This fortress dates from the very end of the Middle Ages
and is one of the last examples of military architecture
(late 15th Century)
built during the same period as Ussé,
Langeais, and Le Plessis-Bourré.*

Wonderful Loire Valley Castles

HISTORY

Pierre de Refuge, Governor of Finances to Charles VII and, later, to Louis XI, built the castle we see today (1475-1483) on the foundations of an earlier castle that had belonged to his family. They were to remain the owners of the castle on this site until the 17th Century. In 1789, it was purchased by the Lambet family who set up a spinning-mill there. It was bought by the State in 1932.

The inner courtyard with its low gallery resembles the Charles d'Orléans Wing in Blois.

TALES AND ANECDOTES

The moat, which has now been filled in, used to be filled by the waters of the Bièvre which was diverted from its normal course towards the chapel by the Lambets when they set up their spinning-mill in the castle.

ARCHITECTURE

A traditional fortress. Machicolated curtain walls encircle a central courtyard. The most attractive part of the architecture is the delightful gallery on the left-hand wing, which has the same form as the Charles d'Orléans Wing in Blois, in front of St. Calais' Chapel.

A close-up of the neo-Gothic decoration on the dormer windows overlooking the lower gallery.

Late 15th-century rafters.

Gien

*This castle belonged to Anne de Beaujeu, daughter of Louis XI and Regent of the kingdom until the future Charles VIII,
whom she married to Anne of Brittany, came of age.*

OUTSTANDING FEATURES

*The inner façade is decorated with strange,
unusual geometric figures picked out in brick
which are still a subject of controversy. The castle, however,
is best-known as the largest museum of hunting in France,
with a number of outstanding, famous works of art
produced by animal sculptors and painters.*

Wonderful Loire Valley Castles

HISTORY

This is the castle that Anne de Beaujeu had built between 1484 and 1500. Anne was Louis XI's daughter and she was very like her father in character. When ruling the kingdom as Regent, she showed wisdom and firmness despite the revolt (1485-1488) led by Louis II d'Orléans, the future Louis XII, whom she imprisoned for a period of three years before her brother, the future Charles VIII, reached his majority (1483-1491). She also arranged the marriage of Charles with Anne of Brittany. She married Pierre II de Bourbon, Lord of Beaujeu.

Decoration on the interior wall: the strange Solomon's seal.

The inner courtyard.

TALES AND ANECDOTES

The inner façade of the castle has one unusual decorative feature - a harmonious layout of red and black brickwork. The bricks, though, form decorative motifs such as a star with six branches, Solomon's seal, three overlapping cards, and a hopscotch. The difficulty of interpretation of the decoration has aroused the curiosity of researchers because it is thought that there may have been a link with the journeymen's lodges which were a characteristic feature of mediaeval society.

A bronze in the inner courtyard.

15th-century rafters in the room given over to the works of the artist François Desportes.

The Falconer (bronze, 19th Century).

ARCHITECTURE

The main characteristic of this building is the pre-Renaissance architecture. The castle has been very well restored after suffering bomb damage in 1940. It was never a mediaeval fortress; it was a stately home although not yet a Renaissance house. It provides a foretaste of the Louis XII Wing in Amboise.

HERITAGE

This is the largest hunting museum in France and it covers all forms of the sport i.e. falconry, trapping, riding to hounds, and shooting. The word "hunting", though, should not be allowed to discourage visitors. This is, on the contrary, an attractive place containing a wealth of artistic treasures, all of them of outstanding interest. Beneath the magnificent 15th-century rafters is a room devoted to the famous artist who specialised in paintings of royal hunts and hounds in the days of Louis XIV - François Desportes.

The museum has a unique collection of 80 sketches and paintings such as the *Dog pointing at Game with a Bouquet of Flowers*, a splendid composition. There are also works by Jean-Baptiste Oudry such as *The Wild Boar Hunt* (18th Century). There are bronzes of animals by Barye, Frémiet, Caïn, Moignez, and P.J. Mène. The museum has an original pen and brown ink drawing by Stradamus (16th-century Flemish School) tinted with white and entitled *Stags behind a Hide* (used to approach game). There is a unique

collection of 4,000 Hunt buttons with the animal hunted picked out in relief and the motto of the Hunt. Other collections include powder flasks, and dog collars with spikes to ward off wolves. There is a splendid collection illustrating the changes and developments of hunting weapons, laid out in chronological order. 15th-century stonebows and stirrup crossbows. Wheelock arquebus. Matchlock musket. Rifle (1862) from Napoleon III's gun cabinet with silver and gold inlays.

A painting by Jean-Baptiste Oudry: The Boar Hunt *(18th Century).*

Langeais

The wall overlooking the courtyard with its three orthogonal staircase turrets.

OUTSTANDING FEATURES

*Viewed from the outside, this is a fortress with a working drawbridge;
seen from the courtyard, it is a Renaissance castle.
The Siegfried family has left us a superb collection of 16th-century furniture
that creates a unique atmosphere from one room to the next.
There is also a valuable collection of tapestries,
most of them made in Flanders.*

The small drawing room: a Madonna and Child on a gold background *(late 13th Century, Sienese School).*

HISTORY

The castle was built in 1465 by Louis XI's Controller of Finances, Jean Bourré who, in 1468, was to go on to commission the building of Le Plessis-Bourré. Its interior was laid out by François Dunois, cousin of the King and son of Joan of Arc's favourite companion-in-arms. The latter negotiated the marriage of Charles VIII and Anne of Brittany which took place in Langeais on 6th December 1491. The marriage was to be political, strategic and military, linking Brittany to France on a permanent basis. To this end, the marriage contract stipulated that if the King died without leaving a male heir, Anne would marry his successor. This was what happened seven years later when she married Charles d'Orléans who reigned under the name Louis XII.

The outer wall. The entrance across the drawbridge with counterweight.

TALES AND ANECDOTES

Anne found herself sole heir to the Duchy of Brittany at the age of 14. A wealthy match such as this aroused a great deal of intrigue. Maximilian of Austria, for example, who was heir to Burgundy, succeeded in marrying the duchess by proxy and his representative symbolically put his leg beneath the sheets of Anne's bed on the evening after the contract was signed. However the Regent of France, Anne de Beaujeu, had the marriage legally annulled in favour of her young brother. The royal spouses were united in a political marriage but they enjoyed six-and-a-half years of a love match until the sovereign's accidental death. They had three sons, all of whom died when little more than babies.

The interior contrasts with the military-style exterior.

ARCHITECTURE

From the outside, the castle looks like a huge, mighty, uniform fortress, a perfect example of 15th-century military architecture. The exterior has a roofed parapet walkway with machicolations supported by trefoiled brackets running along a length of 130 metres. The towers are built in a layout typical of 15th-century military architecture. The lower section projects beyond the upper one, and there are powder magazines as in Le Plessis-Bourré, Brissac and Ussé. Entrance to the castle is by way of a recent drawbridge with counterweights. The walls overlooking the courtyard are less massive thanks to the presence of three orthogonal staircase turrets. There are dormer windows with large gables and ogee arches with crockets and finials. The brackets are decorated with oak leaves, vines, and cabbages. At the end of the park are the remains of one of the oldest

A tapestry in the royal bedchamber.
Aurora and the four signs
of the zodiac *(Bruges, 1530).*

stone-built keeps in France, like the one in Loches (early 11th Century), both of them built by Fulk III Nerra, Count of Anjou. Inside are Renaissance State rooms, all of which have been restored. Magnificent 15th-century rafters can still be seen in the chapel.

HERITAGE

Crucifixion Room - A tapestry of Christ on the Cross flanked by the Virgin Mary and St. John (Brussels, late 17th Century to a design thought to be by Roger Van der Weyden). The extensive use of silks gives an impression of relief and a particularly luminous quality to the work. In the background is Jerusalem,

apparently with slate roofs. There is also a tapestry of the wild queen coming out of the woods (15th Century, Switzerland or Alsace) riding a lion and followed by a man of the woods. In the background is a castle.

Birthwort Room - Three splendid birthwort tapestries with wide-

The Marriage Room: an oak door carved with the coats-of-arms of France and Brittany (15th Century).

leafed climbing plants (Audenarde, 16th Century). They are verdures, although the greens have turned blue now that the yellow ingredient has disappeared.

Marriage Room - Seven out of a series of nine tapestries depicting the nine knights on horseback, each accompanied by two men-at-arms. The Biblical scene shows David and Joshua. Hector, Alexander, and Caesar represent Antiquity; King Arthur and Godefroy de Bouillon illustrate the Middle Ages (16th Century). This theme had been widely used since the 14th Century. Each tapestry bears a caption in French.

Blue Chamber - The Autumn tapestry is one of a series of four (Tournai, late 15th Century). In the centre is an apple tree with tiny figures climbing up it. Around it are a vine branch and grapes. The scene includes men hunting and a couple

eating and drinking. At the top left is a village; to the right is a castle.

Royal Chamber - The tapestry illustrates dawn and four signs of the zodiac (Aries, Gemini, Cancer and Leo). It was made in Bruges in 1530. This is a very modern piece of work which would not be out of place in the 20th Century both as regards the forms and the various shades and hues which are exceptionally well-preserved.

Chapel - Three tapestries (Audenarde, 16th Century) - *The Creation of Adam*, *The Creation of Eve* and *The Temptation of the Serpent*.

Green Tile Chamber - Two tapestries from a series of twelve which are now scattered throughout the world (Louvre, Leeds, Boston) but which originally decorated the chancel in Le Ronceray minster in Angers. The first tapestry (16th Century) is a triptych. On the left is Abel's sacrifice while Adam and Eve go about their everyday business. In the centre is Melchisedech in 15th-century armour welcoming Abraham. To the right is an illustration of the Jewish Passover.

Other objects

Marriage Room - Magnificent carved oak door (15th Century). The coat-of-arms of France with the fleur-de-lys and the arms of Brittany with ermines are in the centre of the door. The mid 16th-century credenza has carved columns and panels. Truth and Justice are shown surrounding Venus carved in the

A tapestry in the Blue Chamber. Autumn (Tournai, late 15th Century).

round, holding a shell and leaning against a dolphin. A 16th-century oak chest has carvings of St. Peter and St. Paul at the corners. On the front is the Adoration of the Shepherds and the Magi.

Small Drawing Room - Wooden panel decorated with a Madonna and Child against a gold background (late 13th Century, Sienese School). See also the Green Tile Room. Painted Madonna and Child (15th Century, Flemish School). Luini Chamber. Nativity Scene (fresco by Luini, 1522, Lugarno).

Chapel - St. Anne teaching the Virgin Mary to read (wooden statue, 12th Century). Splendid gilded wooden reliquary (France, 1250) decorated with semi-precious stones. On the side are six Apostles. On one side of the cover are the Foolish Virgins; on the other the Wise Virgins.

Loches

The Collegiate Church of St. Ours (left). The Agnès Sorel Tower, the Old Apartments completed during the reign of Charles VII then the New Apartments built for Charles VIII and completed by Louis XII (right).

OUTSTANDING FEATURES

This mighty mediaeval fortress is, in many historical and architectural respects,
the equal of Chinon. It was here that Charles VII and Agnès Sorel lived out their passionate love
affair and it is here that visitors can now see Agnès Sorel's tomb containing her ashes.
Louis XI lived here as a child and, later, had his terrible prison-cages installed here.
Anne of Brittany's Chapel is a piece of lace work in stone and the castle also contains
the valuable Passion Triptych painted by Jean Fouquet's School (15th Century).

Wonderful Loire Valley Castles

HISTORY

An earlier fortress was built on this site by Charles the Bald to provide protection against Viking invasions. Through marriage, it became the property of Fulk Nerra and his descendents, Counts of Anjou, who were traditionally opposed to the Counts of Blois. However, when Geoffrey Plantagenet, Count of Anjou, married Matilda (1128), the grand-daughter and heiress of William the Conqueror, he became King of England and the Kings of France began to show an interest in the fortress. Philip Augustus obtained ownership of it by negotiating with John, Richard the Lionheart's brother (Richard was older than him and had been kept prisoner after his return from the Crusades). Richard, however, retook the castle and Philip was unable to capture it again until after his death. It then became Crown property (1205). In the 15th Century, the Old Apartments were the residence of Charles VII and his mistress, Agnès Sorel, the first official mistress of a King of France. She was 20 years younger than the sovereign. He received Joan of Arc here in 1429 and she convinced him that he should be crowned in Rheims. The New Apartments were used by Charles VIII and, later, Louis XII and their wife, Anne of Brittany who married each of them in succession. Louis XI spent most of his childhood in the keep and, in later years, he set up his famous "daughters" (iron cages) there, using them to imprison Cardi-

The Passion Triptych *(1485) by Jean Fouquet's School.*
A tempera painting on wood, with layer upon layer of paint.
In the centre is the Virgin Mary who has fainted.

nal Labalue (1469) and the chronicler Commynes who had rebelled against the Regent, Anne de Beaujeu, sister of the future Charles VIII. The chronicler described the iron and wooden cages, the last surviving example of which was destroyed during the French Revolution. The royal prison also accommodated Louis Sforza, Duke of Milan, who was taken prisoner by Louis XII. He created pain-

tings on the walls of his cell to pass the time and inscribed on them "He who is not happy". The wording has worn off over the past twenty years because the stonework has crumbled away. François I received a visit from Charles V of Spain in Loches but the castle lost its glamour when the Queen, Claude of France, died. The Court then left the palace in Blois and settled in the Louvre.

worth respecting her wishes). Agnès' three daughters, all of them illegitimate, were given the family name of their royal father, for the first time in history. They were called Marie, Charlotte and Jeanne de Valois.

ARCHITECTURE

Like Chinon to which it is linked by so many historical events, this castle is a typical example of one of the mightiest mediaeval military fortresses in France, as is evident in the impressive ruins overlooking the town. The huge keep 37 metres high is reminiscent of the one in Langeais which was built at more or less the same period (early 11th Century) and by the same Count of Anjou, Fulk III Nerra. Note the three large buttressed towers (13th Century) with their long slit-windows. They were added by St. Louis to the outer walls (12th Century) that were in a better state of preservation than the inner walls (12th Century). The machicolated New Tower (15th Century) and the Martelet Tower (15th Century) with three storeys built into the rock date from the reign of Charles VII and their famous dungeons turned the fortress into a prison. The Old Apartments, on which building work began under Charles VI and was completed by Charles VII, were to be the King's official residence and the favourite setting for his love affair with his mistress, Agnès Sorel. The north-west wall has several features characteristic of military architecture viz. crene-

Agnès Sorel's tomb (15th Century) with alabaster recument figure. One of the two angels at the chevet.

TALES AND ANECDOTES

Agnès' grave contains an urn with her remains in it. She died in February 1450, probably as a result of puerperal fever after the birth of her fourth child who lived for only six months. She was initially buried in the chancel of the Collegiate Church of St. Ours near the castle, at her own request (she had gifted the sum of 60,000 golden ecus for this purpose but it represented six times the ransom being demanded for Joan of Arc and Charles VII did not consider it

The Franciscans's Gate in the former town walls.

lations, slit-windows, and turrets that were rebuilt in the 19th Century. It is linked to a large corner tower (13th Century) known as the Agnès Sorel Tower because her tomb was to be found there from 1809 to 1970. The two chambers in this wing had no

Anne of Brittany's chapel with her emblem, the Franciscan girdle.

ceiling during the reign of Charles VII. Instead, they were open to the rafters 14 metres above the ground, which explains why the windows were so long for the period. This chamber is famous in the history of France for it was here that Joan of Arc, accompanied by her faithful companion-in-arms, Dunois, is said to have met Charles VII (June 1429) for the second time; the first meeting took place in Chinon. She is said to have convinced the monarch on this second occasion to travel to Rheims for his coronation. He agreed but only on condition that she open the way for him. This led to a series of victories including the Battle of Patay.

The second wing in the New Apartments (late 15th, early 16th Centuries) were commissioned by Charles VIII and completed during the reign of Louis XII. They are reminiscent of the Charles VIII wing in Amboise Castle, with their traceried dormer windows (in this instance, they are topped by pinnacles). Note the carved dogs looking out towards the forest; they indicate that this was once a hunting lodge. The wing contains the remarkable chapel with ogival vaulting used by Anne of Brittany and built during the reign of Louis XII. It has been totally restored. Everything about it serves as a reminder of the queen, including the ermine tails decorating the walls and the emblem of the Franciscan girdle above the altar flanked by traceried stonework as fine as lace. It was planned to include a fireplace, a highly unusual feature in such a place, although there is also one in St. Hubert's Chapel in Amboise.

HERITAGE

Joan of Arc Chamber - Audenarde tapestry (17th Century). Verdure with trompe l'oeil effect. A path leads off to the right-hand side, but seems to lead to the left if you stand on the right side of the tapestry. Agnès Sorel's tomb (15th Century), an alabaster recumbent figure on a black marble base with two angels beside her head and two lambs at the foot symbolising Agnès. Passion triptych by Jean Fouquet's School dating from 1485, during the reign of Louis XI. *A tempera* painting on wood, with layer upon layer of paint. It is estimated that the work took between 10 and 12 years to complete. It was a piece of team work with each artist subject to different influences. The hills have been painted in a style reminiscent of Florentine art; the 15th-century costumes show the Flemish influence (Van Eyck, Van der Weyden). The huge horses, one of Fouquet's specialities, might be the work of the master himself. There is an amazing amount of realism in the work, visible in the unconsciousness of the Virgin Mary, the drops of blood at the dead Christ's mouth, and the plants at his feet - they are all different. Initials at the bottom right, near a monk in prayer, are those of the donor. This is a quite outstanding work showing a profusion of images, a sense of perspective, and inimitable shades of green.

Le Lude

To the left are the huge mediaeval towers with Renaissance decoration built for Jean Gendrot, King René's overseer of building work (1520-1530). To the right is the Louis XVI façade consisting of a building in three parts designed by Jean Barré, the architect of Montgeoffroy.

OUTSTANDING FEATURES

*This castle attracts attention for the diversity
of architectural styles dating from the 15th to 18th Centuries,
the frescoes (16th Century) in its chapel and the 18th-century interior
decoration (wainscoting, furniture, and tapestries).*

The Angel of Le Lude
(bronze, 15th Century).
The hallway with coffered ceiling
bearing the coat-of-arms and
monogram of the Daillon family.

HISTORY

In the 10th Century, faced with the threat of Viking invasions, the Fort de la Motte was built. In the 13th Century, it became a stone fortress and the property of the Counts of Anjou. During the One Hundred Years' War, it was captured by the Count of Warwick (1425) and freed by Gilles de Rais (1427). Jehan de Daillon, Chamberlain to Louis XI, purchased it in 1457 and began to restore it. His descendants continued to live in it until 1685, altering it so that it gradually reflected changing styles in architecture. The refurbishment and alterations then continued in the 18th Century after it was purchased by Mr. Du Vehaer (1751), a partner in the East India Company. With his niece, the Marquise de la Vieuville, he was the ancestor of the current owners and restoration work continued throughout the 19th and 20th Centuries.

The music room.

TALES AND ANECDOTES

The Marquise de la Vieuville cunningly gave some of the furniture to the revolutionary authorities in Angers in order to avoid the ransacking of the castle. During restoration work in the 19th Century, the 17th-century tapestries from the dining room and 16th-century wainscoting that decorated the bedchambers were discovered beneath parquet flooring.

*Paintings in the chapel, by Primaticcio's studio
(15th Century).*

Ogival vaulting.

ARCHITECTURE

The main characteristic of Le Lude is its architectural diversity. There are four main styles present here - the Gothic façade, the inner courtyard, the Louis XVI building and the main entrance.

The Gothic façade still has its system of defence with huge towers, a parapet walkway and machicolations. However, its "Italian Renaissance" refurbishment, which was undertaken between 1520 and 1530 by Jean Gendrot, overseer to the Good King René of Anjou, gave it a dazzling finish. A three-arched terrace links the mediaeval towers containing mullioned windows flanked by pilasters and decorated with a double string-course emphasising the various storeys. Tall traceried dormer windows in an Italianate style counterbalance the series of Classical medallions decorating the façades - this is a major decorative feature of the castle. The inner courtyard, which is shaped like a horseshoe, is typical of the French Renaissance because of its symmetrically-placed features. The Louis XVI façade linking the north and south wings was built (1787) by the architect Jean Barré, who designed the castle at Montgeoffroy. It is remarkable for the orderly layout of its various features. The central section, topped by a triangular pediment, stands out from the wings and has a symmetrical layout of niches and medallions. The entrance is flanked by two towers linked by a Louis XVI portico.

The main drawing room.

HERITAGE

A 16th-century medallion.

Foot of the grand staircase - *The Angel of Le Lude* (15th Century, bronze).

Gallery in the North Wing - 16th-century chest decorated with the Daillon coat-of-arms.

Blue Drawing Room - Furnished and includes 18th-century Beauvais tapestries. 16th-century Flemish cabinet with drawers decorated with fine paintings by Otto Van Weilen, Rubens' teacher.

Grand Drawing Room - Louis XVI wainscoting, 18th-century gilded wood furniture. 18th-century Gobelins tapestry. Case containing personal effects belonging to Marie-Antoinette. Chapel, 16th-century frescoes depicting scenes from the Old Testament. Ceiling with ogival ribs. Drawings bear the hallmarks of Primaticcio's studio. French-style gardens.

Meung-sur-Loire

The mediaeval towers.

OUTSTANDING FEATURES

This is a historically-important fortress that was once the seat of the Bishops of Orléans
(11th - 18th Centuries). Thanks to the research and enlightened restoration
work undertaken by the present owner, it is now an amazing example of 12th- and 13th-century
military architecture. Be sure not to miss the underground passages
to the dungeons where the poet Villon was imprisoned. They are significant examples
of the savagery of the mediaeval justice system.

HISTORY

This castle belonged to 59 bishops and 6 cardinals of Orléans from the 11th Century to the French Revolution. Liphard, Governor of Orléans, entered holy orders and lived here, in a low-roofed room within the castle that had been razed almost to the ground by the Vandals (5th Century). He died in 550 A.D. and was canonised; his grave was found near the collegiate church. In 1101, Lionet, Lord of Meung, rebelled against the Bishop of Orléans and was besieged by royal troops. He had to leap out of the keep, which was on fire, with his troops; they fell onto spikes set up below. The castle has a bloody past and, in the Middle Ages, it was used to imprison bishops and State prisoners. Lord Salisbury, the Commander-in-Chief of the English forces, died here in 1428. After the capture of Orléans, the English army returned in haste to Meung which was then attacked by the Duke d'Alençon and Joan of Arc. She spent two months here. The mediaeval poet, Villon, was imprisoned in the castle but was set free by Louis XI who was charmed by a poem which he thought had been written in praise of himself. Henri IV had the course of the Loire changed so that it flowed past the foot of the castle. In the 18th Century, Sextius Jarente, a bishop in disgrace, lived in the castle. He, like his nephew at a later date, gave lavish receptions that attracted many famous people of the day.

The bishops' bathroom, showing the 17th-century bath.

TALES AND ANECDOTES

During the French Revolution, the bishop hid a solid gold statue of St. Liphard in the castle. The bishop was beheaded and the statue has never been found. The dungeon, 12 metres deep and 5 metres in diameter, was rediscovered in 1973 by the present owner, beneath a fake hillock that had probably been built in the

The entrance to the dungeons was concealed in the 18th Century and has only recently been rediscovered.

never put in the dungeon. Instead, he was imprisoned in an underground cell and subjected to water torture. Five litres of water were poured into the prisoner, swelling the stomach, and he was then tied upside down for 24 hours against the wall of his cell. The swelling gradually subsided but the acompanying pain was excruciating. At the foot of a staircase in the main apartments is a trapdoor opening onto a well 17 metres deep. A system concealed in a cupboard beneath the stairs was used to open and close the trapdoor.

A sedan chair.

A rare armchair with X-shaped legs (15th Century). The Gothic ornamentation has been added.

park in the 18th Century, in an attempt to conceal, as much as possible, all reminders of a dark past. Since bishops could not commit murder without infringing the commandment, "Thou shalt not kill", they used to let condemned prisoners down into the dungeon on a rope and there they died very quickly in the absolute darkness. One jug of water and one loaf were provided every day, whatever the number of prisoners. In the centre of the dungeon is a well, designed for human excrement; the weaker condemned prisoners were also thrown down it by their stronger cellmates. Villon was found guilty of aggravated theft but was

Wonderful Loire Valley Castles

ARCHITECTURE

Many of the buildings in the old castle date from the 12th or 13th Centuries. The pink pebbledashed wing overlooking the main courtyard (17th Century) was restored. Beneath the 12th-century towers are 11th-century dungeons which were rediscovered after having been walled up in distant times. They were found still to have their shackles and iron doors. There is an underground chapel (12th Century) which was used as a refuge; it has a dry well and a larder. At the top of a spiral staircase in one of the towers, the joist framing of the chestnut wood rafters (13th Century) is supported on 15th-century brackets representing the symbols of the Evangelists. The guardroom has the only Y-shaped ogival vault in a vernacular building in France. The bishops' bathroom is rather strange. It has a 17th-century bath at floor level, gouged out of the rock in the Roman style. The taps are shaped like swans' heads. Behind the wall is the copper which provided the hot water.

Underground passages dating from the 11th to 12th Centuries.

The Jansenist representation of Christ by Jacob Van Dyck.

HERITAGE

Jansenist figure of Christ by Jacob Van Dyck. The arms are almost vertical and the fingers point up to heaven. An armchair with X-shaped legs decorated with two eagles; it dates from the period of William the Conqueror and has a Gothic backrest which was a later addition. There are numerous tapestries (Aubusson and Flanders, 17th Century).

78

Montgeoffroy

The central apartments with forepart flanked by wings with a pavilion set at right angles. To the right is St. Catherine's Chapel (16th Century).

OUTSTANDING FEATURES

*Montgeoffroy has all the charm of a large 18th-century stately home laid out
with architectural symmetry. It is also one of only three castles in the Loire Valley
to have retained its original furniture handed down from one generation of the family to the next.
Those who have a particular fondness for the Louis XV style will be delighted with their visit,
especially when they see one of the first dining rooms in France.*

A restored stained-glass window (16th Century) in the chapel.

HISTORY

The Montgeoffroy estate belonged to Geoffroy de Châteaubriand (1209), ancestor of the great French writer, then to the de la Grandière family (16th Century) before being sold to Erasme de Contades (1676). His descendent, Louis-Georges-Erasme de Contades was given command of the Rhine Army in 1758 and raised to the rank of Maréchal. Later, he was appointed Governor of Alsace (1762) and lived in great luxury in Strasbourg. He expressed a wish to retire from military affairs at the age of 68 and had this castle built (1772-1776). He lived through the French Revolution, totally unscathed.

TALES AND ANECDOTES

The castle and its furniture were protected by Hérault de Séchelles, member of the Convention, who spent his childhood here with his mother, Madame de Séchelles.

ARCHITECTURE

The castle is built in the shape of a horseshoe. There is a central section with forepart, and pavilions set at right angles to it, each with its wing. Montgeoffroy still has two large towers (16th Century) from the previous castle and the Gothic chapel dedicated to St. Catherine that was built by Guillaume de la Grandière (1543). It is the symmetrical layout of the 18th-century façade and its overall sense of balance that catch the eye. The forepart, for example, is based on the figure '3', with three

The set of copper pans in the superb castle ktichens (16th Century), which are still used today.

One of the first "dining rooms" still in existence (18th Century) with the Strasbourg ceramic stove purchased by the Maréchal de Contades.

storcys, a large triangular pediment decorated with the Maréchal's coat-of-arms, triangular decoration above the great bay windows on the ground floor and three semi-circular French windows. Symmetry is the main feature in the layout of the tall, slender chimneys and circular dormer windows to each side of the pediment. The impressive façade is balanced by the elegant pavilions including the same architectural features as the forepart.

HERITAGE

Billiard Room - Portrait of Louis XIII which was a gift from the monarch himself. Two tapestries (Aubusson, 18th Century) depicting episodes from the story of Anthony and Cleopatra.

Blue Drawing Room - Portrait of Louis XIV after Rigaud. It was a gift to the Maréchal's father from the sovereign.

State Drawing Room - Finely carved wainscoting that is typical of the Louis XVI style. Similar panelling can be seen in the music room in Valençay. The room contains a very rare pair of square-backed two-seater bergères.

Drawing Room - Eight French Regency armchairs and two sofas from the same period. Portrait of Hérault de Séchelles at the age of 7.

Square Drawing Room - 6 Louis XV armchairs covered with their original tapestry "with carnations and grapes". 4 Louis XV chairs with period tapestry. 2 Louis XV chests of drawers, signed by the cabinetmaker. Madame de Séchelles' dressing room still has its period wall coverings. Red damask bedchamber. Rosewood bonheur-du-jour from the reign of Louis XV. Louis XVI marquetry table.

Dining Room - One of the first chambers to be known as a "dining room"; the fashion was introduced at the end of Louis XV's reign. Paintings. Two superb still lives with dog and game by

The Blue Drawing Room with the portrait of Louis XIV after Rigaud. The painting was a gift from the monarch.

Desportes. Portrait of Louis XV by Van Loo. Louis XV chairs with wide seats and narrow backs to facilitate service. Ceramic stove from Strasbourg, a gift to the Maréchal. Superb kitchens (16th Century). 18th-century kitchen table. 260 pieces of copper and pewter plate.

Chapel - Wonderful stained-glass window (16th Century with restoration) depicting God surrounded by the angel musicians, singers and the symbols of the four cardinal Virtues.

Le Plessis-Bourré

The architecture of this castle, which was built in the late 15th Century, is decidedly mediaeval with its terrace on which cannons could be placed in order to strafe attackers.

OUTSTANDING FEATURES

Access to this castle is not always easy but it is well worth making the effort because this is one of the Loire Valley's greatest castles, and a "must" on any tour. It was built in just five years of uninterrupted work at the end of the 15th Century and has remained unchanged ever since, surrounded by a wide moat in an age-old setting. Its architecture is pleasantly uniform and the castle is well-furnished. It also contains one of the most mysterious gems of the 15th Century i.e. the ceiling in the guardroom, which is painted with symbolic and moralising scenes at the request of Jean Bourré, Treasurer to Louis XI, who was said to dabble in alchemy.

Wonderful Loire Valley Castles

HISTORY

The estate was purchased (1462) by Jean Bourré, Grand Treasurer to Louis XI, Captain of Langeais, and Governor to the heir to the throne, the future Charles VIII. The castle was built from 1468 to 1473 and was visited by Louis XI while on a pilgrimage to Notre-Dame de Béhuard. In 1487, it was the turn of Charles VIII and Anne de Beaujeu, Regent of France, who met Hungarian Ambassadors in the reception room known as the "Parliament Chamber". The castle was bought from the Bourrés by the de Ruillés in 1750 and sold in 1850 to the Weiss family, who are still the owners today.

TALES AND ANECDOTES

The coffered ceiling with its symbolic messages (1480) was skilfully hidden from sight in 1750 in order to conceal scenes that might be considered as shocking. This was fortunate since it saved this treasure during the tormented days of the French Revolution. The beams are decorated with the coats-of-arms of the House of Anjou, J. Bourré and King René.

Top: *The coffered ceiling in the guardroom. It was concealed in 1750.*

The ceiling in the guardroom: a thin she-wolf only devours faithful wives (late 15th Century).

ARCHITECTURE

The castle was built as a family fortress and visitors had to cross three drawbridges before reaching the entrance. The walls are thick and the castle includes slit-windows, a keep and corner towers. The architecture is, then, mediaeval in style. It has not undergone any alterations and is still typical of the second half of the 15th Century. The innovatory feature was the terrace round the castle, on the edge of the moat, where guns could be placed in order to fire at ground level. Inside, the buildings, doors and windows are more harmonious, with an arcaded gallery closing off the courtyard. The apartments have tall, mullioned windows with narrative brackets and dormer windows decorated with coats-of-arms (France, J. Bourré and King René). The guardroom and reception room have their original flooring (15th Century) of Anjou earthenware tiles. The King of France's Staircase, which has a strange grotesque, leads to the reception room with an Anjou Gothic vaulted ceiling and a 15th-century fireplace decorated with a row of triangles. Some people believe there is a connection with alchemy.

Top: *A man throwing a stone into a well, splashing himself with water. This symbolises the need to think before acting (late 15th Century).*

A monkey riding an elephant symbolises the need for mind over matter (late 15th Century).

HERITAGE

The ceiling in the guardroom is of outstanding interest. On the coffers and beams is painted, without any apparent order and sometimes set head to tail, a succession of small, vividly-coloured scenes that demand a certain amount of thought, given the subject matter. There is, for example, a monkey riding an elephant which may represent mind over matter. Some of the paintings are humorous, such as the man throwing a stone into water and soaking himself in the effort; others are cynical, such as the skinny she-wolf that only feeds on women who are faithful to their husbands.

The furniture is also outstanding because the castle has always been lived in. It includes three superb drawing rooms (French Regency, Louis XV, and Louis XVI) with magnificent 18th-century carved wainscoting.

Maréchal Soult's Bedchamber (Empire style) - The tapestries depict the Acts of the Apostles (Brussels, 17th Century). There is a verdure from Aubusson. Art work includes two pastel drawings by Quentin Latour.

The inner courtyard with arches linking the apartments to the chapel.

State Drawing Room - Mazarin desk (Boulle, 17th Century).

Reception Room - 15th-century Flamboyant Gothic doorway with a superb lock decorated with the coat-of-arms of France.

Guardroom - The sculptures include St. Martin sharing his cloak (limestone, 15th Century), Joan of Arc with her hands tied (15th Century), and Charles VIII on horseback wearing a crown (15th Century).

Church - St. Anne, the Virgin Mary and the Infant Jesus (16th Century). Outstanding life-sized statue of the Mater Dolorosa (15th Century). Very fine Pietà (15th Century). Carved choirstalls (16th Century).

A full-length representation of Charles VIII (wood, 15th Century).

Joan of Arc with her hands tied, flanked by her enterprising torturers (wood, 15th Century).

Reception room: an outstanding lock decorated with the coat-of-arms of France (15th Century).

Saumur

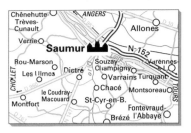

The murmuring waters of the Loire flow gently beneath the walls of Saumur Castle.

OUTSTANDING FEATURES

It is difficult not to be enchanted by this elegant castle reminiscent of the town's famous military riding school, the Cadre Noir. It also calls to mind the illuminated manuscript that depicted it in the 15th Century; its outline has changed very little since then. It contains priceless collections of mediaeval enamelware, mediaeval wood carvings and mediaeval tapestries and an outstanding, instructive exhibition of 16th-19th century ceramics. There is also a Horse Museum.

Wonderful Loire Valley Castles

HISTORY

The castle built on a feudal motte and given to Gelduin by Eudes II, Count of Blois, was captured by Fulk III Nerra. Recent archaeological digs have revealed the remainder of a stone-built keep dating from the 12th Century. The castle was later captured from King John of England by Philip Augustus (1203) and, c. 1230, St. Louis turned it into a fortress. Louis I of Anjou, King Charles V's brother, rebuilt a castle that can be seen in the miniature called *Les Très Riches Heures du Duc de Berry* (early 15th Century). His grandson, the Good King René, turned it into a pleasant residence in the late 15th Century; it was used by Charles VII. It became a Huguenot fortress governed by Duplessis-Mornay, companion-in-arms to the future Henri IV. During the French Revolution, Cathelineau was elected Supreme Commander of the Catholic Army in the courtyard here. It was used as a State prison in the 18th and 19th Centuries.

A platter from the Bernard Pallisy School (late 16th Century).

The inner courtyard: the well with its hoist (13th Century) and the three-storey grand staircase with its Flamboyant Gothic decoration. Recent digs carried out in the courtyard revealed the remains of a "keep" built in the 12th Century. This was probably the "Castrum Salmurum".

TALES AND ANECDOTES

English seamen, taken prisoner in the 18th Century, have left graffiti on the walls.

ARCHITECTURE

The lower section of the towers is circular (12th Century, part of the castle commissioned by

The climb up to the fortified bartizan leading to the inner courtyard.

St. Louis) with tufa bonding that is almost square. The towers are octagonal with more elongated bonding (14th Century, dating from Louis I of Anjou's castle). The 16th-century ramparts are reminiscent of Vauban's designs but were erected one century earlier to designs by Bartholomeo, an Italian architect, working to a commission from Duplessis-Mornay. A barbican with two corbelled lookout towers leads into the courtyard. Visitors then cross the former guardroom which still has its fireplace. In the courtyard, there is a 15th-century pavilion with grand staircase. It has three storeys decorated in the Flamboyant Gothic style and is reminiscent of Chaumont. The 13th-century well still has its hoist. The north-west wing was demolished, as it was in Ussé, Villandry and Chaumont.

HERITAGE

It was Count Lair, the generous donor from Saumur, who gave the castle its priceless collections of Limoges champlevé enamelwork (12th-13th Centuries), painted Limoges enamelware (16th-17th Centuries), small woodcarvings from Germany, Flanders, Britain, Spain, and France (13th to 18th Centuries), and the outstanding collection of ceramics. In addition to the 16th-century majolica ware and late 16th-century dishes from the Bernard Palissy School, the exhibition retraces the history of glazed earthenware through the ages, from imitations of Chinese porcelain (Nevers, Rouen, 17th Century) to the

St. James (Nevers faïence).

"radiating" styles with symmetrical decoration and Rococo designs with lace-type edges. The 17th-century pieces from Moustiers, Montpellier, Marseilles, Sceaux, and Strasbourg include "potato" decoration. The soft

St. Catherine of Alexandria, a statue that used to stand in a niche in the Queen of Sicily's House in Saumur (oak, Loire Valley School, 15th Century).

The tapestry entitled Children Gardening, after sketches by Lebrun and Desportes (Manufacture Royale des Gobelins, c. 1718).

porcelain from Sèvres, Chantilly and St. Cloud was a first attempt at reproducing Chinese porcelain but it scratched and was not translucent (early 18th Century). The collection also includes 17th and 18th-century Chinese porcelain, the first porcelain to be produced in Meissen after the discovery of kaolin seams in Germany (early 18th Century) and the first French porcelain (late 18th Century) made after the discovery of a kaolin seam near Limoges. Other outstanding items include a tapestry entitled *The Dance of the Savages* (Arras, 15th Century), and another called *The Capture of Jerusalem*

(Arras, 15th Century). There is a complete series of 18th-century Gobelins tapestries that have kept their vivid colours and are entitled *The Child-Gardeners*. They depict the four seasons and may have come from Ménars Castle which belonged to the Marquise de Pompadour. Note, too, the superb oak statue of St. Catherine of Alexandria (France, 15th Century) with finely-carved hair. The Horse Museum is worth a visit.

A reliquary in the shape of a chapel. The figures etched into the copper and then gilded stand out against the enamelled background (13th-century technique, Limoges). This is an example of champlevé work.

Serrant

The main courtyard and the buildings set out in the form of a horseshoe. On the sides are pavilions built of schist. Note the layout of the façades with their firepots, the lantern turrets above each tower and the central section topped by a pediment (15th - 18th Centuries).

OUTSTANDING FEATURES

*This castle is outstanding for its external and internal architecture
(16th and 17th Centuries). It houses one of the finest collections of original furniture
which is both refined and varied.
The Empire pieces are of particular interest as is the private library,
one of the most extensive in France.*

Wonderful Loire Valley Castles

Antoine-Philippe de la Trémoïlle,
*Commander-in-Chief of the cavalry
of the royalist rebel army.
A portrait by Guérin.*

*The moat and one of the towers
which are identical to the ones in
Valençay.*

HISTORY

The estate belonged to the Serrants until the 14th Century when it passed to the Brie family. Charles de Brie built the central apartments in 1546, along with the stables and the dovecote. The estate then changed hands several times, belonging at one point to the Bautru family (1676). Guillaume de Bautru, Marquis de Vaubrun, was killed during a glorious cavalry charge at Altenheim (1675) shortly after Turennes. His wife was inconsolable and she had him buried in the chapel. The castle was sold to the Walshes, a family of Irish extraction, in 1749; they were fervent supporters of the Stuarts. François-Jacques Walsh was made a French Count by Louis XV (1755). One of his descendants married the Duke de la Trémoïlle (1830) and his family are still the owners of the castle today.

TALES AND ANECDOTES

Louis XIV and his courtiers were on their way to Nantes to arrest Fouquet, Intendant of Finances, when they became bogged down in the mud on the paths near the castle. Napoleon Bonaparte, the Duchess de Berry and Napoleon III were also visitors to the castle. Empress Josephine was godmother to Valentine Serrant whose mother, Louise de Vaudreuil, was a friend and lady-in-waiting of Her Imperial Majesty.

The superb library.

ARCHITECTURE

The horseshoe-shaped castle is surrounded by a moat. The grand courtyard between two schist pavilions that form a stark contrast to the white tufa façade is closed off by a wrought-iron grille bearing the Walsh coat-of-arms with the "desolate swan". Note the orderly layout of the façades on which the windows are flanked by rows of pilasters (16th Century). There are firepots along the balustrade and they, like the two huge towers topped by lantern domes, are reminiscent of Villandry. All the bedchambers in the towers have basket-handle or semi-circular coffered ceilings. The designs were by Philibert Delorme, the architect who provided the plans for Fontainebleau. The inner staircase, consisting of two flights with landing, is similar to the one in Chenonceau as regards the beauty of its coffered vaulting decorated with various stylised flowers. The chapel, designed by Hardouin-Mansart (1680) who was the architect of Versailles, contains the white marble mausoleum of the Marquis de Vaubrun, carved by Antoine Coysevox.

A carved ebony cabinet.
A close-up of the interior with its painted landscapes.

Tapestry: Animals from a fantasy world *(Brussels, early 17th Century).*

HERITAGE

Dining Room- 7 tapestries (Flanders, Audenarde, 17th Century) on the theme of Ovid's *Metamorphoses.* The painting showing Antoine-Philippe de la Trémoïlle commanding the cavalry of the Royalist army is by Guérin.

Prince de Tarente's Bedchamber - The room contains two very rare Regency corner cabinets in kingwood (a tropical wood that is purple in colour). The painting shows Louis XIII as a child (17th Century).

Princess's Bedchamber - The Louis XVI clock incorporates the phases of the moon. The Louis XV marquetried desk is an early form of filing cabinet. It has its own clock (a unique piece). The chest is attributed to Boulle - it has copper, silver and tortoiseshell inside and out. The Louis XIV chest of drawers shows very early marquetry work. The Louis XVI dropleaf desk was designed to enable people to write standing up. The enamelled wood chest (16th Century) is decorated with figures showing the Creation of Eve, the Temptation, and Adam and Eve being chased out of the Garden of Eden.

Library - One of the most priceless private collections in France, consisting of 12,000 rare volumes including Diderot's *Encyclopaedia of Sciences* (1751). There are also incunabulae, books published by the Elsevier family, a collection of engravings by Piranesi, and stories by La Fontaine with the original etchings by Fragonard. Also included is a first edition of the discovery of Egypt by the scientific mission led by Bonaparte and a trictrac board made by Jacob. The double escritoire can be adjusted to suit the height of its user (Empire period). On the Louis XVI mahogany desk, each wing is a escritoire in its own right and has its own inkwell. There is also a central escritoire.

State Drawing Room - 8 magnificent tapestries of a quality rarely seen (Brussels, early 17th Century) representing imaginary animals. Each tapestry has its own theme, e.g. Good (represented by an elephant) combatting Evil (represented by a dragon). There is a famous carved

ebony chest with ivory inlays (late 14th Century) attributed to Jean Macé with landscapes inside. This is an absolutely outstanding piece of furniture. The Empire Bedchamber has mahogany period furniture and a bust of Empress Marie-Louise by Canova. The castle contains a painting by Gérard, *The Duchess de Rohan* and a superb charcoal drawing by Desportes entitled *Dogs in front of a Pair of Pheasants* (17th Century).

Top: *The Empire bedchamber.*

The great dining room.

Sully-sur-Loire

The 14th-century keep (left) encircled by the moat filled by the R. Sange and two of the towers which lost their upper storeys. In the centre is the keep, the Renaissance wing where Sully had his apartments and the entrance pavilion. To the right are the two towers in the curtain wall, one of which partially demolished while the other one was left intact.

OUTSTANDING FEATURES

*This is a charming mediaeval fortress surrounded by a moat and a vast park.
It is steeped in memories of the last moments of semi-freedom enjoyed by
Joan of Arc before she was taken prisoner. There are also memories of Sully,
the minister to Henri IV famous for his wisdom. The very fine series of tapestries on the theme
of Psyche is one more example of the extraordinarily fine tapestries in the Loire Valley castles.*

Wonderful Loire Valley Castles

HISTORY

The estate belonged to the Barons de Sully from the 10th to the 14th Centuries (1381) when it was bought by Guy de la Trémoïlle, who commissioned the main features in the castle we see today. His son, Georges, Chamberlain to Charles VII, was a mere tool in the sovereign's hands and he held Joan of Arc here under what might be called "house arrest" after the king's coronation and the defeat at La Charité-sur-Loire. She escaped and fought the Burgundians who then took her prisoner at Compiègne. She was burnt at the stake in Rouen on 30th May 1431. In 1620, Maximilien de Béthune bought Sully and Henri IV raised it to a duchy. One of his descendants received a visit here from Voltaire.

The Duke's bedchamber

TALES AND ANECDOTES

The Duke retired to the castle at the end of his life and wrote a book glorifying Henri IV's reign and describing the work that he himself had achieved with the monarch. It was called *Memoirs of the wise and royal economies of State*. It was printed in one of the castle towers (1639-1640) by a printer from Auxerre. The young Voltaire who had written two satirical pieces about the Regent was exiled to Sully (1716). He was to return often thereafter, because he had met Mademoiselle de Livry who was involved in the entertainments given at the castle. Among other things, she staged some of the plays written by the author.

ARCHITECTURE

The keep is a mediaeval fortress (14th Century) with 4 corner towers, a parapet walkway, machicolations and a series of vast chambers one above the other (they measured 300 sq. metres and 100 sq. metres) with impressive fireplaces. The small castle (14th Century) is built over a porch-tower and contains Sully's apartments. An 18th-century wing, which has been restored, was a gallery in Sully's day linking the castle to the keep. The oak rafters in the keep are 35 metres long and 15 metres high; they are among the finest rafters produced in the 14th Century.

There is no main truss. Instead, there is a series of king beams supporting rafters, an innovation in its day and still something of a surprise today.

HERITAGE

A series of 6 tapestries (Paris, 17th Century) illustrating the mythical tale of Psyche, a young beauty of whom Venus was jealous.

State Room - There is a strange iron door (16th Century) concealed behind the wainscoting. It leads to the room from which the drawbridge could be raised or lowered and in which the Duke de Sully used to store his treasure. The tomb of Sully and his wife is a copy; the original is in Nogent-le-Rotrou.

Duke's Bedchamber - Superb French ceiling painted "in the Italian style", depicting the gods on Mount Olympus.

Rafters in the keep (14th Century) built in the shape of an upturned boat.

Talcy

The austerity of this keep flanked by corner turrets comes as a surprise,
given that it was built in the early 16th Century for a Florentine banker.

OUTSTANDING FEATURES

This house belonged to a wealthy Renaissance banker and it has a secret life all of its own for,
although it has not been lived in since 1932, there is always a feeling that the owners
will be coming into view any minute. This atmosphere may be due to the outstanding collection of
furniture in every room, in particular the 17th-18th century chairs, many of them very rare pieces.
The castle was the home of Cassandra, the subject of a poem by Ronsard, and Agrippa d'Aubigné
fell ill here but was tended back to health by Diane, the woman who was in love with him.

Wonderful Loire Valley Castles

HISTORY

Bernard Salviatti, a Florentine banker, bought the estate in 1517. He had a daughter, Cassandre, whom the poet Ronsard noticed during a ball given in Blois by François I (1545). The poet never came to the castle but he sang the praises of the beautiful young girl in his famous *Ode to Cassandra*. Jean, Cassandra's brother, had a daughter, Diane Salviati, who was betrothed to the poet Agrippa d'Aubigné. During the Wars of Religion, Jean welcomed to the castle King Charles IX, then aged 12, and his mother, Catherine de' Medici, the host's cousin, who organised the so-called Talcy Conference (June 1562) in an attempt to bring together the protagonists. The conference was attended by the King of Navarre, the Prince de Condé and Coligny. The St. Bartholomew's Day massacre was to take place 10 years later. General Chanzy spent one night in the castle (11th December 1870) when the French troops retreated back across the Loire.

TALES AND ANECDOTES

Ronsard could not have married Cassandre because he was an Oblate, i.e. he had received the first tonsure. She was married to a wealthy nobleman at the age of 15. Agrippa d'Aubigné, one of the Huguenot leaders, was wounded in the Beauce region and sought refuge with Diane who cared for him for three weeks. Jean Salviati, her father, who was a liberal Roman Catholic, agreed to their marriage but one of her uncles, who was a Knight of the Order of St. John of Malta, vetoed it. Diane died shortly afterwards, apparently of a broken heart. Cassandre's daughter married Guillaume de Lutsen, an ancestor of poet Alfred de Musset. Agrippa d'Aubigné was an ancestor of Madame de Maintenon, a bigoted Roman Catholic and the last wife of Louis XIV.

A 16th-century gallery with surbased baskethandle arches like the ones in the Louis XII Wing in Blois.

ARCHITECTURE

Although he was an Italian, Salviati did not have his castle built in the fashionable Italianate style of the day. Instead, he preferred austerity. He obtained permission to have the tower fortified on condition that it was not used for defensive purposes. Late Gothic motifs can still be seen in the door surrounds and beside the windows on the lower level. It was a stately home, described in archives as the "Residence and farm of Talcy", and it was built for a wealthy middle class owner, not an aristocrat. The most interesting architectural feature is the 17th-century gallery with sur-based basket-handled arches, like the Louis XII Wing in Blois. It still has traces of paintwork that might date from the Renaissance period, for it was painted in Italian ochre. The well (16th Century), dovecote (16th Century) with two revolving ladders and the 17th-century wine press in perfect working order are three outdoor features which are an essential part of the property. Inside, the servant's hall has a French-style ceiling (16th Century) on which the main beams are decorated with cable moulding, balls and festoons.

The Great Drawing Room with its complete collection of Louis XV seats, all of them bearing the same cabinetmaker's stamp.

HERITAGE

Rare mille fleurs tapestry (15th Century) from the Loire Valley workshops. This is a variation called an "emblematic mille fleurs" because it has the coat-of arms and initials of the donors in the centre.

Antechamber - Rare, Louis XIV gilded wooden chairs. Louis XIII chair with arms decorated with carvings of ladies in ruffs. The "armchair" did not appear until c. 1640.

Chanzy Bedchamber - Roman-style bed dating from the days of the Napoleonic Empire, with a tester in the shape of a tent. This is a reference to Bonaparte's Egyptian campaign. Very rare desk-washstand (18th Century). The drawers are divided off into compartments for letters. There is a dressing-table at the top with a retracting mirror and spaces for rouge pots. There is also a jewellery drawer and a retracting bidet made of Rouen faïence. The built-in soap dish is lined with metal to protect the wood.

Reception Room - Louis XV armchairs stamped with the Lelarge mark and upholstered in Aubusson tapestry. The medallion backs are decorated with biblical or mythological figures.

Small Drawing Room - 6 Louis XV armchairs stamped by the same cabinetmaker (they are rare items). Louis XV curved-front commode-tombeau reminiscent of Classical sarcophagi. The decoration is Rococo with gilded bronzes. Their func-

A rare millefleurs tapestry full of emblematic significance (15th Century).

tion is both aesthetic and practical, as they provide protection in the places most easily-damaged.

Dining Room (18th Century) - Square Louis XV seats bearing the Belet stamp. The wall covering is 18th-century painted East India Company cloth hung on battens.

State Drawing Room - The drawing room contains a rare, complete set of Louis XV seats bearing the same cabinetmaker's mark and including square-backed chairs, cabriolet armchairs, bergère chairs, a straight-backed settee and a basket settee. There are also Louis XV tables with rounded corners designed to fit snugly against candlesticks. Aubusson tapestries (17th Century) depicting the love of Venus and Adonis, and the birth of Bacchus. Louis XV chest-of-drawers bearing the Desmoulin stamp and said to have belonged to the Duke

de Choiseul. It is decorated with vernis Martin, a technique which competed with Chinese lacquer that could only be applied overseas.

A very rare secretaire.
A wash-stand (18th Century).

Ussé

To the left is the east wing (15th Century) that was refurbished by the de Bueil family. In the centre is the south wing built in the 16th Century over an older gallery. The west wing (16th Century, right) was built by the d'Espinays. Set at right angles to it are the 17th-century apartments with the keep in the background.

Outstanding Features

Given the fairytale appearance of this castle, it comes as no surprise to learn that it inspired the story of The Sleeping Beauty written by Charles Perrault, nor that Chateaubriand, with whom the lady owner was in love, came to write here. The castle contains a range of valuable works of art e.g. Teniers tapestries and majolica ware from Faenza.

HISTORY

Jean V de Bueil, one of Charles VII's principal lieutenants, rebuilt a fortress on the site of an older stronghold that had originally been held by Gelduin, Lord of Saumur and much-feared enemy of Fulk III Nerra. Jean's son, Antoine de Bueil, was married to Jeanne, the daughter of Charles VII and Agnès Sorel. He sold the castle to the d'Espinays who improved it and sold it in 1659 to the Marquis Bernin de Valentinay whose son married the heiress of Maréchal de Vauban. In the 19th Century, the castle belonged to the Duchess de Duras and Countess de la Rochejacquelin.

A close-up of the carved statues (Jean Goujon School, c. 1535).

The collegiate church (early 16th Century) with its Italianate decoration.

A 16th-century Florentine cabinet with 49 drawers inlaid with mother-of-pearl and ivory.

TALES AND ANECDOTES

Charles Perrault, a friend of Mr. de Valentinay, came to the castle and his visit is said to have inspired him to write *Sleeping Beauty*. Many of the rooms in the attics are reminiscent of the fairytale. Le Nôtre, another of Mr. de Valentinay's friends, is said to have laid out the terraced gardens. The Duchess de Duras had a literary salon in Paris and was, for many years, in love with Chateaubriand who apparently wrote some of his *Memoirs from Beyond the Grave* there and gave the duchess the cedar trees near the collegiate church. He called her "my dear sister" and she wrote to a friend that she was acquainted with all the pain of love without ever enjoying its advantages.

The Madonna and Children: Jesus and St. John the Baptist.
A piece of Florentine ceramic made for Lucca Della Robbia.

East Wing: a dormer window that has undergone extensive restoration.

ARCHITECTURE

From the outside, this castle resembles a mediaeval fortress that is, in some ways, reminiscent of Langeais. It has the same corbelled parapet walkway topped with towers and an upper storey set back from the line of the remainder of the tower. The drawbridge used to be flanked by two towers facing each other. Projecting beyond the

Tapestries by Teniers (close-up).

façade is the apse of the former chapel with its three buttresses. The North Wing used to overlook the gardens but it was demolished in the 18th Century, when parts of other castles such as Chaumont and Villandry were also destroyed. From the courtyard, it is obvious that the apartments form a pleasant residence which contrast with the mediaeval appearance of the exterior. The South Wing (15th Century) has a gallery and its appearance can be imagined from the ribbed arch in the south-east corner which was altered early in the 16th Century by the addition of dormer windows between the buttresses and in the 17th Century by the addition of large windows on the upper storeys and French windows on ground level. The east wing is pleasant enough but it was disfigured by restoration work in the 19th

Century with the exception of the hexagonal lantern turret with Flamboyant Gothic archivolts (15th Century). The dormer windows in the west wing are Renaissance in style. There are some superb rafters in the attics. The early 16th-century collegiate church stands at the eastern end. It bears the initials of the people who commissioned the building, a "C" for Charles D'Espinay and an "L" for Lucrèce de Pons, his wife. This is a Gothic building with pinnacled doorway and buttresses, but its decoration is Classical.

HERITAGE

Guardroom - The tapestry is a verdure (Aubusson, 17th Century). There is a rare collection of Saracen weaponry (18th Century). The gallery is outstanding and the Teniers tapestries are unusually fresh and vivid (Flanders, 18th Century). They depict scenes from country life and village fetes. The majolica vases come from Paenza (16th Century).

Drawing Room - The 16th-century tapestry illustrates the battle between David and Goliath. The Florentine cabinet (16th Century) with 49 drawers is inlaid with mother-of-pearl and ivory.

King's Bedchamber - Louis XVI tester bed set along the wall rather than projecting from it. The walls are hung with a rare salmon-pink silk decorated with Chinese motifs (18th Century). In the other rooms, there are period costumes illustrating a different theme every year.

Chapel - Superb carved choirstalls (16th Century) by Jean Goujon's School. The Florentine ceramic by Luca Della Robbia depicts the Virgin Mary with the Infant Jesus on Her lap.

South Wing: the Teniers Tapestry Gallery (18th Century).

Valençay

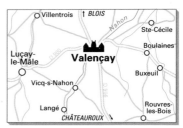

*The main courtyard. From left to right: the neo-Classical façade known as the "Louis XVI"
with its fluted pilasters and firepots, the domed West Tower, the arches and the keep.*

OUTSTANDING FEATURES

*The majesty of this impressive Renaissance castle is as surprising as the domes on its towers.
The full glory of the 17th Century can be seen in the courtyard where the style is resolutely
neo-Classical. The lavish interior is full of memorabilia relating to the Prince de Talleyrand,
like an unchanging moment in time. However, when the wily diplomat came to Valençay,
he brought with him the atmosphere of the Napoleonic Empire and it is evident through
the vast apartments. As to the tapestry called* **The Bulls** *(Gobelins, 17th Century),
it is a delightful masterpiece but only one among the many contained in the castle.*

The Blue Drawing Room: a portrait of Talleyrand at his desk, by Gérard.

HISTORY

There used to be a mediaeval castle on this spot then the estate was purchased by Robert III d'Etampes, Chamberlain to Charles VII (1451) and it remained in his family until 1766 when it was sold to financier John Law. Successive owners extended and embellished the castle but the best-liked of them all was arguably Achielle d'Etampes Valençay. He was a Knight of the Order of St. John of Malta and he fought the Turks before entering the service of Louis XIII and taking part in the Siege of La Rochelle as a vice-admiral. He later became Captain of the Guard to Queen Marie de' Medici. He was made a cardinal by Pope Urban III. Napoleon bought the castle but gave it to Mr. de Talleyrand who became the most famous of all the personalities in the castle's history -

and he is buried there. During the Spanish War, the King and his family used the castle as their residence.

TALES AND ANECDOTES

Talleyrand was very close to the Duchess de Dino, his nephew's wife. She ruled the household and the castle received visits from the most famous people of the day including Balzac, George Sand, Turner, Guizot and, the greatest celebrity of all, Thiers whom the skilled diplomat trained for a political career.

The King of Spain's Bedchamber.

The Blue Drawing Room: a Boulle desk and oak wainscoting with carved garlands.

ARCHITECTURE

The most surprising characteristic of the façade is the keep, which is majestically highlighted by a postern gate that was one of the military features of the feudal castle. It is a supreme example of Renaissance architecture, including all three Orders - Doric, Ionic and Corinthian, the same Orders seen on the three floors in Chambord.

The Grand Drawing Room in which the seats are decorated with tapestry made in Saint-Cyr stitch by the ladies of the King of Spain's Court. The table was used for the Congress of Vienna (1815).

The Périgord Study: a mahogany desk that was a gift from Murat.

Above them, though, is a graceful frieze of machicolations on brackets carved with foliage and grotesques, left-overs from the Middle Ages. This shows a determination to provide protection against marauders, and the drawbridge could be raised if necessary. Despite this, it is the towers in Valençay which attract attention because of their slightly Byzantine domes, added for aesthetic reasons. There is only one other example of this type of architecture, in Serrant. The West Tower dates from the 16th Century and is, therefore, older than the East Tower built in the 17th Century to counterbalance the other one. Overlooking the courtyard is one of the largest Neo-Classical façades in France known as the Louis XVI Façade. It is beautifully proportioned with fluted pilasters topped by Ionic capitals and laurel wreathes plaited with ribbons. In the centre is a helianthemum, the symbol of the sun. Above them is a frieze consisting of small cubes, in the imperial style. At roof level, there are alternating tall, French-style windows, the firepots that were a symbol of a high-ranking residence (they can also be seen on the terraces in Versailles) and a bull's eye window. On the lower storeys, the façade is broken up by the arches that were not walled up in the days when Talleyrand lived here.

The main staircase: a close-up of The Bulls *(Gobelins, 18 th Century).*

HERITAGE

Ground-floor Gallery - Armchairs and sofas dating from the end of the 18th Century.

State Drawing Room - 26 seats upholstered in tapestry made using the Saint-Cyr stitch by the ladies-in-waiting to the King of Spain during his exile and given to Talleyrand. The painting is a full-length portrait of Prince de Talleyrand by Prud'hon. The large round table was used for the signing of the Treaty of Vienna in June 1815.

Blue Drawing Room - Ferdinand signed the Treaty of Valençay here, putting an end to the Franco-Spanish War in December 1813. Talleyrand liked to work here. The Boulle desk is inlaid with tortoise-shell and copper. The portrait of Talleyrand at his desk is by Gérard. The music room is representative of the Louis XVI style, with its garlands carved in the oak panelling and its portraits of young girls in the Classical style.

Talleyrand's bedchamber - The room contains the bed in which Talleyrand died (in Paris) and a glass cabinet containing his medals and decorations.

King of Spain's Bedchamber - Early 19th-century wallpaper printed using blocks and representing episodes in the life of Psyche.

Bénévent Bedchamber - The room contains a particularly fine portrait of the Princess de Bénévent by Madame Vigée-Lebrun. There is also a pair of Louis XVI bergère chairs and a Regency chest-of-drawers bearing the Duval stamp.

Périgord Study - The superb mahogany desk has fluted columns and winged female sphinxes. It was a gift to Talleyrand from Murat. The marble busts of Voltaire and J.J. Rousseau are by Houdon.

Grand Staircase - There is a graceful white marble statue of Ariadne of the Vatican. Hanging on the wall is a marvellous brightly-coloured tapestry full of intricate detail called *The Bulls* (Gobelins, 18th Century, part of the "New Indies" series) made to designs by the animal painter Desportes.

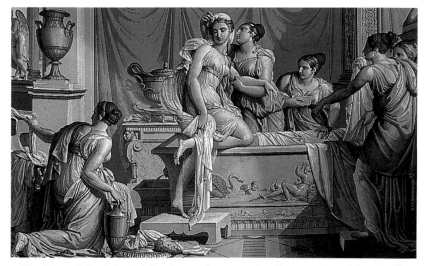

The King of Spain's Bedchamber: a close-up of wallpaper painted in grisaille and representing a scene from the life of Psyche.

The main staircase: a white marble statue (Ariadne of the Vatican).

Villandry

Foreground: the formal gardens. Background (left): the decorative vegetable garden; (right) the Seville garden and castle.

OUTSTANDING FEATURES

This Renaissance castle is world famous for its gardens i.e. the decorative vegetable garden which recreates the art of 16th-century gardening through its combination of vegetables and flowers, the Seville-style garden and its ornamental symbolism, and the formal French garden. Inside the castle is an amazing Hispano-Moorish ceiling and a collection of paintings by the Spanish and Flemish Schools bequeathed by Dr. Joachim Carvallo, the enlightened owner who undertook the restoration of castle and gardens.

Wonderful Loire Valley Castles

HISTORY

It was in the mediaeval fortress, of which the keep has survived (it can be seen from the gardens) that the Peace Treaty of Colombiers was signed by Philip Augustus and Henry II Plantagenet who died a short time later in Chinon. Jean le Breton, Secretary of Finances to François I, had the present castle built and it remained in his family until 1753. It then passed to the Castellanes. In 1906, it was purchased by Dr. Joachim Carvallo, who was born in Spain where he studied medicine. He came to Paris and worked with Professor Richet, a Nobel prizewinner. He was a freethinker who bought Villandry to set up a research laboratory after marrying one of the richest heiresses in the U.S.A. whom he had met through his work. He very quickly fell in love with the castle and launched an extensive restoration project to give it back the appearance it had had in the 16th Century (it had been disfigured in the 18th). He was militant in his support for the saving of French heritage and set up the *Association des Demeures Historiques* in order to encourage owners to restore their castles and open them to the public. He was converted to Roman Catholicism, as was his wife, and the gardens that he created are an expression of his philosophical and religious beliefs.

The main courtyard, East Wing: a dormer window with carved gable.

TALES AND ANECDOTES

Dr. Carvallo was a lover of Spanish art work and he acquired an extensive collection that has since been dispersed as a result of legacies and successions. In an auction sale in Toledo, he bought an absolute gem - the ceiling of a mosque. After the Spanish Conquest, a number of Christian details were added and these additions are clearly visible. They include scallop shells, and the coats-of-arms of Spanish families.

ARCHITECTURE

The buildings form a horseshoe around a grand courtyard, as they do in Villesavin. The arcades round the cobbled courtyard give the building an ethereal appearance which is seen again in the dormer windows with their carved gables in the Renaissance style. The façades are broken up by decorative pilasters that are covered in ornamentation from the base of the arcades up to the dormer windows. The lack of symmetry introduced by the slightly closed angles between the central apartments and the two wings creates an element of surprise that has its own special charm.

The main courtyard, East Wing: the arches.

THE GARDEN

There are three gardens. The first of them is a vegetable garden, the second is a flower garden and the third is a formal French-style garden. The vegetable garden is a descendant of mediaeval monastery gardens when plants were gathered in various geometrical forms based on the symbol of the Cross. The influence of the Renaissance after the Italian Campaign led to the addition of flowers such as petunias and begonias. In the vegetable garden today, there

West and south walls, showing the keep. This is the view from the vegetable garden.

are two crops every year, one in spring, planted in mid-March and removed in mid-June. All the early crops are removed to leave space for the summer and autumn crops of simple vegetables which existed during the Renaissance and which give

The Seville-style Garden of Love.

The colours in the vegetable garden vary depending on the season. This is the descendant of mediaeval monastery gardens.

various splashes of colour. They include different varieties of cabbage, leeks, Swiss chard, celery, pumpkins, aubergines, and tomatoes. The colour of the vegetables varies a great deal from one season to the next, giving a multi-coloured checkerboard effect. Every year, some thought has to be given to the plants that will be used to give good colour harmony and form while complying with the horticultural constraints of the three-course system. This means that the same variety of cabbage will not be planted in the same bed for three years so that the soil does not lose all its nutrients, even though fertiliser is used. It is important to fill the beds well and ensure that the plants are all healthy. The best period to enjoy the variety of colours is early in September when the dahlias are in bloom in the vegetable garden and the best time of day is the evening at about seven o'clock when the sun is low in the sky. The second, ornamental garden, is of Arabic inspiration with box, yews and dahlias. An artist from Seville designed it, taking as his inspiration the gardens of Granada. He developed the symbolism of Love. Tenderness is symbolised in the masks, and Love broken by Passion in the spikes of the red dahlias. The third, formal French-style garden is separated by box hedges instead of trellis fencing as it was in the 18th Century.

The ceiling from a Spanish mosque.

St. John the Evangelist
(Goya's School).

HERITAGE

Paintings : *Assumption of the Virgin Mary* (17th Century, Murillo's School). *Country Loaf* (Zurburan's School, 17th Century). *A Young Boy in his Sick-bed* (Goya's School). *St. John the Evangelist* (Goya's School). *The Dice Players against a Landscape* (Ribera's School). *Judas' Kiss* (Flemish School, 17th Century). *Nativity* (Flemish School, 17th Century). *The Ascension* (Flemish School, 17th Century).

Villesavin

*Left to right: the moat along the front of the house, the east pavilion containing the chapel,
the main courtyard, the front of the apartments with five bays flanked by pilasters, and the west pavilion.*

OUTSTANDING FEATURES

*Villesavin may have been built by the same designers
who worked on Chambord nearby, especially as its owner, Jean Breton,
was close to François I and monitored the work undertaken on the great royal residence.
It is strange, indeed, to see such grace and harmony in an
Italianate residence hidden in the depths of the forest.*

Wonderful Loire Valley Castles

HISTORY

Jean Le Breton, the son of a nobleman, was taken prisoner at the Battle of Pavia (February 1525) and shared the captivity of François I in Spain. On his return, he was named Lord of Villandry, Secretary of the King's Finances and Administrator of the County of Blois. More importantly, he became responsible for the Chambord Building Project. He took advantage of the know-how of the Italian artists present to have his own stately home built close by, from 1527 to 1537. François I paid him a visit here, in particular in 1541 two years before Jean le Breton died. His wife, Anne Gédouin, and his daughter, Léonor, were then appointed to govern Chambord. Villesavin later belonged to Jean Phelipeaux who received Marie de' Medici, widow of Henri IV, and the young Louis XIII there.

TALES AND ANECDOTES

When Jean Phelipeaux had the paintings finished on the ceiling of the chapel in honour of Marie de' Medici's visit, the most noteworthy part of the work was the miracle of St. Veronica's veil. However, it is not Christ's face that is shown vaguely outlined on the piece of cloth; it is the face of the castle owner. The impressive dovecote next to the house is also open to the public with its original solid oak ladder. This is no mere "pigeon loft", a symbol of lower and middle-ranking justice; it is a "fuye", a dovecot that was a symbol of the highest echelons of the judicial system who were entitled to mete out capital punishment.

ARCHITECTURE

The castle is built in a horse-shoe shape, with one upper floor overlooking the main courtyard. There is a moat along the front. The courtyard is lined with two pavilions backing onto the moat. They have tall dormer windows, showing that the attics were habitable. The east pavilion contains the chapel; the west pavilion includes the guardroom which is linked to the central apartments by a building with superb Renaissance dormer windows topped by pediments decorated with human figures such as a comedian, musician etc. The east pavilion is separated from the main apartments by a wall decorated with medallions depicting Roman emperors; they came from Bologna. The main apartments are broken up by the five bay windows flanked by pilasters and topped by gilded dormer windows.

Above: Marble basin (XVIth).

A fresco in the chapel.

The dovecot with its original ladder.

HERITAGE

Marble basin (16th Century, Lombardy).

Chapel - Early 16th-century frescoes depicting the Scourging of Christ, and the Entombment. Early 17th-century frescoes. Marie de' Medici's chapel painted with black veils as a sign of mourning.

Interior - Superb chest (late 16th Century). Fine Louis XIII table. Museum of horse-drawn carriages.

Additional Sightseeing

The strange bell-tower in the monastery (Grand-Moûtier) looks down, eight hundred years after it was first built, on the silent footfalls of respectful tourists as they pass beneath the arches in the cloisters.

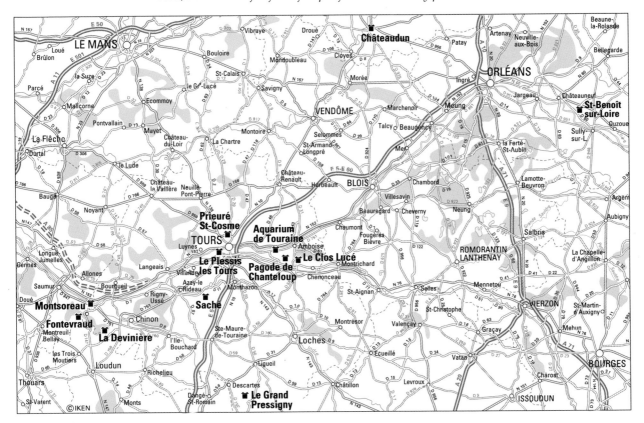

FONTEVRAUD

Outstanding Features

This is an impressive, breathtaking abbey, a place of historical research and archaeological digs, and not by any means a castle of course. But what an abbey! It was governed by abbesses appointed from among the royal family and all of them have left their mark on the place where many a king, queen, prince, and nobleman, especially from among the reigning family in England, came on a spiritual retreat and chose as their final resting-place. It is a remarkable piece of 12th-18th century architecture that was rediscovered in later years and subjected to admirable restoration work. Because of this, it fully deserves its place in any description of places of historic and architectural interest in the Loire Valley.

History

In 1101, Robert d'Arbrissel, an ascetic and fervent preacher, denounced the vice that was prevalent at the time and settled, with his followers, in a valley in the depths of the forest, near the point where the River Evrault rises. There he founded a monastery which quickly grew in size and importance. At the end of his life, he entrusted its running to an abbess who was responsible for a community of nuns and a community of monks, a quite unique situation. The abbey enjoyed the protection of the Counts of Anjou

The Roman-esque kitchens (exterior).

they are still continuing. The abbey has housed the Centre Culturel de l'Ouest since 1975 and the Comité d'Histoire Fontevriste since 1991.

Tales and Anecdotes

The minster chancel contains the graves of the abbesses but, to the right of the high altar, a dig revealed the sarcophagus of Robert d'Arbrissel who died on 7th March 1116.

Architecture

Entrance Courtyard - 18th-century stables. Abbess' lodgings.

Inner Courtyard - Minster. The nave has four restored domes (they date from the 12th Century) like the cathedral in Angoulême. The arches and pendentives are supported on square pillars backed by double columns with narrative capitals. The transept has barrel vaulting like the chancel and is topped by the bell-tower supported on tall pillars with engaged columns. The chancel contains the stone tombs (early 13th Century) of Henry II Plantagenet, his wife Eleanor of Aquitaine, and their son Richard the Lionheart, and the wooden tomb (mid 13th Century) of Isabelle of Angoulême, wife of John Lackland. The main monastery (16th Century) has Renaissance cloister galleries except on the south side where they are of Gothic design. The mid 16th-century chapter house has vaulting resting on graceful colonettes. The 16th-century calefactory has been restored. The long refectory (16th Century) has thick 12th-century walls and Gothic vaulting. The dorters have been restored. The staircase to the dorter consists of a straight flight of 35 monumental steps. St. Benedict's infirmary (16th Century) and its 12th-century chapel were built in the Plantagenet style. St. Lazarus' Priory has

i.e. Fulk and his sons and their descendant Henry II Plantagenet, who had his son, John Lackland, brought up and educated here. Henry II mounted the throne of England but was buried here, in the abbey, in 1189. The abbey church then became the burial place of 15 princes and princesses of the family that reigned in England where priories attached to the parent community of Fontevraud spread as quickly as they did in France and Spain (12th Century). Abbess Mary of Brittany (1457-1477) reformed the Order, giving it new impetus and an influence that led to the construction of a large number of the buildings that visitors can see and admire today. The abbey was later run by abbesses from

the royal family of Bourbon (1491-1670) and the royal abbey took on a more worldly and intellectual character without losing any of its spirituality. Abbess Gabrielle de Rochechouart de Mortemart (1670-1704) had Racine's play, *Esther*, staged here; she also opened the abbey's doors to her sister, Madame de Montespan, who had fallen into disgrace. The abbey's intellectual influence and its aristocratic seemliness led Louis XV to entrust it with the upbringing and education of his daughters (1738). In 1792, the nuns were forced to flee, the furniture was sold off and the abbey became a prison (1814-1963). Since then, major archaeological digs and restoration projects have been undertaken, and small cloisters which were restored in the 17th Century and a 12th-century chapel in the Anjou Gothic style. The refectory in the South Wing dates from the 17th Century. The famous Romanesque kitchens (12th-century interior) have a central octagonal fireplace and side rooms containing side fireplaces. The calefactory houses a terracotta Pietà dating from the 17th Century and made in Le Mans, in the workshop of Charles Hoyau. Among the paintings on wood is a 16th-century Crucifixion showing Christ between the two theievs and, kneeling at the foot of the Cross, Louise de Bourbon, Abbess of Fontevraud (1534-1575).

Heritage

Chapterhouse - 16th-century black and white pavement bearing the initials of the abbesses Louise and Renée de Bourbon, the Bourbon shield and the salamander that was the de Valois emblem. The walls are decorated with 16th-century paintings showing scenes from Christ's Passion and portraits of the abbesses.

Mediacval gardens.

St. Michael's Church in the village has a superb high altar brought here from the abbey.

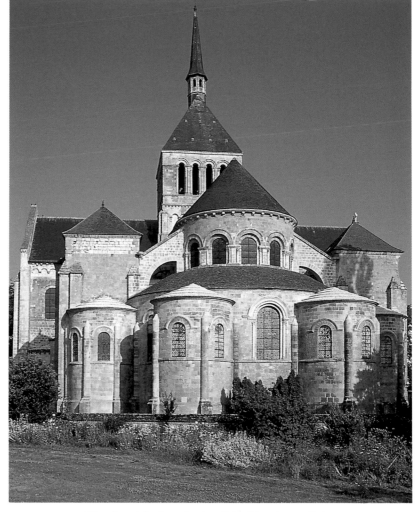

The chevet in the minster, Saint-Benoît-sur-Loire.

ABBEY, SAINT-BENOÎT-SUR-LOIRE

The abbey crypt, Saint-Benoît-sur-Loire

The abbey was founded in 650 A.D. and housed St. Benedict's relics. This was one of the leading monasteries of its day, with a brilliant cultural life, especially during the Carolingian period and until the 11th Century. It was destroyed during the French Revolution and only the superb minster (now restored) survived. Its 11th-century tower-porch, which was of Carolingian inspiration, is eye-catching for its square layout, and its two storeys with three windows on each side. The narrative capitals are characteristic of Romanesque architecture, as are the chancel, 11th-century transept and 12th-century nave.

ST. COSME PRIORY

The priory was set up in 1092 by the collegiate church of Saint-Martin-de-Tours for five canons. Ronsard was a commendatory prior here in the 16th Century and was buried in the priory. His skull was found at a later date and is now buried in a grave covered with rose bushes. All that remains of the 11th-century church restored on the orders of Louis XI are one arch, three chapels and an ambulatory with some outstanding narrative capitals. The prior's apartments date from the 17th Century.

The abbey chancel.

The ruins of Ronsard's priory.

Architecture by Seignes (late 15th Century): Le Plessis-les-Tours.

LE PLESSIS-LES-TOURS

Only one, rather modest wing (late 15th Century) remains of the vast fortified castle rebuilt on the orders of Louis XI (1475) where the king shut himself up in fear of conspiracies. Its brick architecture is a reminder of the fashion for this type of construction, prevalent in the Loire Valley in the late 15th Century. Other examples of it can be seen at Le Clos-Lucé and Gien.

A model built according to Leonardo da Vinci's sketches (paddle steamer).

LE CLOS-LUCÉ

Built in 1477 for Etienne le Loup, Master of the Royal Household under Louis XI, the residence now consists of only one brick building, with 19th-century extensions. Charles VIII purchased it and had the chapel built. There are still traces of three frescoes (recently restored) by pupils of Leonardo da Vinci. The great artist lived here from 1516 until his death on 2nd May 1519. The house contains forty amazing models built by I.B.M. to the sketches made by the great man whose wonderful imagination produced, for the first time, a tank, an aeroplane, a swing bridge, a helicopter etc.

Wonderful Loire Valley Castles

The brick-built Clos-Lucé.

SACHÉ

This 16th-century manor house with 18th-century alterations belonged, in the 19th Century, to Mr. de Margonne, a friend of Balzac's mother. The author made the house famous by staying there on many occasions for some considerable time between 1829 and 1837. He wrote *Louis Lambert* here and, more importantly, *The Lily of the Valley* in which he described the countryside round about. Numerous documents and interesting manuscripts are now displayed in the museum.

Balzac enjoyed staying here.

LA DEVINIÈRE

This house, now restored, was the birthplace of Rabelais.

Rabelais' birthplace.

MONTSOREAU

This is a superb example of military architecture, built by Jean de Chambes, Counsellor to Charles VII (1450), and it still has its battlements. The façade overlooking the inner courtyard is remarkable for its 16th-century east turret on which the windows are richly decorated. It contains a very fine staircase with fan vaulted roof. The dramatic events that have been recorded in history (the murder of the Lord de Bussy, the lover of Françoise de Maridor, Lady of Montsoreau and wife of Charles de Chambes, the instigator of the St. Bartholomew's Day massacre in Anjou) did not occur here but in another castle lower down the valley. It no longer exists.

Montsoreau Castle (15th Century) overlooking the Loire.

CHÂTEAUDUN

This was the residence of the famous Jean Dunois, Joan of Arc's favourite companion-in-arms, who won glory during the reconquest of the country during the reign of Charles VII and obtained the highest honours of the day, culminating in 1465 in the removal of the strip on his coat-of-arms indicating that he was illegitimate. He rebuilt the castle between 1451 and 1468. All that remains is a circular keep 31 metres high with 15th-century fireplace and rafters. The Holy Chapel is decorated with some remarkable 15th-century statues and what is thought to be a statue of Dunois himself. Other

A 15th-century statue.

noteworthy features include the façade on the Dunois Wing, the great spiral staircase with loggia-type landings and the Longueville Wing including a grand Italianate staircase.

A fresco: The last Judgement.

The façade of Dunois Castle.

Other Places of Interest

Grand-Pressigny: the keep.

The pagoda.

THE CHANTELOUP PAGODA

Built on piles between 1775 and 1778, this pagoda 40 metres high has six storeys linked by wonderful wrought-iron steps. It was given to the Duke de Choiseul by his friends from the Court who used to pay him visits at his castle (it no longer exists) after he had been sent into exile by Louis XV.

LE GRAND-PRESSIGNY

This castle is famous for its superb Renaissance gallery and the extensive collections in its Prehistory Museum.

TOURAINE AQUARIUM

This is the largest freshwater aquarium in Europe and is interesting from an aesthetic and educational point of view.

Historical Figures, Museums and Architecture

Below is a thematic list of historical figures and items that are considered as part of France's heritage and have some connection with the buildings described in this work (the list is open-ended).

HISTORICAL FIGURES

Anne of Brittany: Langeais, Chinon, Loches, Amboise, Blois

Anne de Beaujeu: Gien, Langeais, Le Plessis-Bourré

Agnès Sorel: Chinon, Loches, Ussé

Joan of Arc: Chinon, Loches, Sully

Eleanor of Aquitaine: Chinon, Fontevraud

Balzac: Saché

Jean Bourré: Langeais, Le Plessis-Bourré

Charles VII: Chinon, Loches, Amboise

Charles VIII: Langeais, Chinon, Loches, Amboise, Le Plessis-Bourré

Charles d'Orléans (Louis XII): Chinon, Loches, Amboise, Blois

Claude of France: Blois

Catherine de' Medici: Blois, Talcy, Chenonceau

Charles IX: Blois, Talcy, Chenonceau

Chateaubriand: Ussé

Diane de Poitiers: Chenonceau

Félix Duban: Blois

Fulk III Nerra: Langeais, Saumur, Loches

François I: Blois, Amboise, Loches, Chambord, Villesavin, Azay-le-Rideau

François II: Amboise

Duke Henri de Guise: Blois

Gaston d'Orléans: Blois

Henry II Plantagenet: Chinon, Ussé, Fontevraud

Henri II: Amboise, Chenonceau

Henri III: Blois

Henri IV: Saumur, Meung, Brissac

John Lackland (King John of England): Chinon, Fontevraud, Angers

Louis IX (St. Louis): Angers, Loches, Saumur

Louis XI: Loches, Amboise, Le Plessis-Bourré, Angers, Le Plessis-les-Tours

Louis XIII: Brissac

Leonardo da Vinci: Amboise, Le Clos-Lucé

Louis XIV: Serrant, Chambord

Louis-Philippe: Amboise

Marie de' Medici: Blois, Brissac

Philip Augustus: Chinon, Loches, Angers

Charles Perrault: Ussé

Richard the Lionheart: Chinon, Fontevraud

René of Anjou: Angers, Saumur

Ronsard: Blois, Saint-Cosmes

Rabelais: La Devinière

Richelieu: Chinon, Beauregard, Brissac

J.J Rousseau: Chenonceau

Sully: Sully-sur-Loire

Talleyrand: Valençay

Villon: Meung-sur-Loire

TAPESTRIES

14th Century: Angers
15th Century: Langeais, Angers, Talcy, Saumur
16th Century: Langeais, Meung-sur-Loire, Angers, Ussé, Blois, Azay-le-Rideau, Chenonceau, Chaumont, Chambord
17th Century: Chinon, Langeais, Loches, Angers, Cheverny, Azay-le-Rideau, Sully-sur-Loire, Serrant, Chenonceau, Le Plessis-Bourré, Chambord, Blois
18th Century: Chambord, Valençay, Ussé, Blois, La Ferté-Saint-Aubin, Brissac
Aubusson, 17th Century: Meung-sur-Loire, Talcy, Chinon
Beauvais, 17th Century: Azay-le-Rideau
Beauvais, 18th Century: Le Lude
Gobelins, 17th Century: Cheverny
Gobelins, 18th Century: Saumur, Le Lude
Paris: Chambord
Teniers (Flanders, 18th Century): Ussé, Cheverny

FURNITURE AND FURNISHINGS

Louis XIV: Cheverny, Beauregard, Azay-le-Rideau, Talcy
French Regency: Montgeoffroy, Cheverny, Valençay
Louis XV: Montgeoffroy, Cheverny, Serrant, Talcy, Brissac
Louis XVI: Cheverny, Serrant, Ussé, Le Lude, Valençay
Empire: Amboise, Serrant, Talcy, Cheverny
Restoration: Amboise
Louis-Philippe: Amboise
Cabinets, 16th Century: Ussé, Azay-le-Rideau, Chenonceau, Serrant, Le Lude
Chests, 16th Century: Amboise, Le Lude, Langeais, Cheverny
Chest-of-drawers, Louis XIV: Serrant
Chest-of-drawers, Louis XV: Talcy, Cheverny, Montgeoffroy
Chest-of-drawers, Regency: Valençay
Kitchens, 16th Century: Montgeoffroy, Beauregard, Villesavin
Armchairs, Louis XIV: Talcy, Cheverny
Armchairs, Louis XV: Talcy (complete collection of drawing room chairs), Montgeoffroy
First dining room, 18th Century: Talcy, Montgeoffroy
Limoges enamelware, 12th - 17th Centuries: Saumur
Statues, 13th - 18th Centuries: Saumur, Beauregard, Le Plessis-Bourré, Chinon, Valençay, Chenonceau
French faïence (glazed earthenware), 17th, 18th, 19th Centuries: Saumur, Chambord
Wall coverings (painted or woven cloth), 18th Century: Talcy, Ussé
Gardens: Villandry, Beauregard, Chenonceau, Fontevraud

PAINTINGS

13th Century: Langeais
15th Century: Langeais, Loches
16th Century: Langeais, Cheverny, Azay-le-Rideau, Chenonceau, Beauregard
17th Century: Cheverny, Chenonceau, Montgeoffroy, Serrant, Brissac
18th Century: Montgeoffroy, La Ferté-Saint-Aubin
19th Century: Blois
Frescoes, 16th Century: Villesavin, Le Lude, Langeais, Fontevraud
Spanish art, 17th - 18th Centuries: Villandry
Flemish art, 17th Century: Villandry

OUTSTANDING
ARCHITECTURAL FEATURES

Mediaeval castles: towers, outer walls
Amboise - Angers - Châteaudun - Chinon - Fougères-sur-Bièvre - Langeais - Le Lude - Le Plessis-Bourré - Loches - Meung-sur-Loire - Saumur - Sully-sur-Loire - Ussé

Flamboyant Gothic
Amboise (Charles VII Wing - St. Hubert's Chapel) - Blois (Louis XII Wing)

Outstanding towers
Amboise (Minims Tower) - Angers (seventeen Flamboyant Gothic towers) - Azay-le-Rideau - Chambord (corners, lantern) - Chaumont (Amboise Tower) - Chenonceau (Marks Tower) - Chinon (Coudray Tower) - Loches (fortified tower, New Tower, Agnès Tower) - Serrant (domed tower) - Valençay (twelve domed towers)

Arcaded galleries
Blois (Louis XII Wing) - Chambord (façade) - Fougères-sur-Bièvre - Le Plessis-Bourré - Villandry - Talcy

Staircases
Angers (vaulting above spiral staircase) - Azay-le-Rideau (flight-on-flight with loggias) - Blois (loggia with Italianate balcony, Gaston d'Orléans Wing) - Chambord (grand double-spiral staircase in the centre of the keep, external François I staircase, external Henri II staircase) - Chaumont (in the octagonal tower) - Chenonceau (interior staircase) - Cheverny (straight flights with landings) - Valençay

Doors
Angers (Count's Palace, 12th Century) - Azay-le-Rideau (monumental entrance) - Blois (St. Hubert's Chapel, exterior, Louis XII Wing) - Langeais (15th Century, Marriage Room) - Meung-sur-Loire (dungeon doors) - Sully-sur-Loire (treasure room)

Outstanding rooms
Ambroise (States General Chamber) - Beauregard (Bell Cabinet, Portrait Gallery) - Blois (States General Chamber) - Chambord (cross-shaped rooms, state room with wainscoting and fireplace that were gifts from Louis XV) - Langeais (Marriage Room) - Le Plessis-Bourré (Guardroom) - Meung-sur-Loire (Guardroom, bishop's bathroom) - Valençay (Talleyrand's bedchamber)

Tiling
Beauregard (Delft) - Blois - Chaumont (majolica ware) - Chenonceau - Le Plessis-Bourré

Coffered ceilings
Azay-le-Rideau (staircase) - Beauregard (Bell Cabinet) - Chambord (cross-shaped room on 2nd floor) - Chenonceau (inner staircase) - Cheverny (King's Bedchamber) - Le Plessis-Bourré
French-style ceilings with decorated beams
Azay-le-Rideau - Cheverny - Le Plessis-Bourré - Talcy

Rafters
Blois - Glen - Langeais - Sully-sur-Loire - Ussé
Symmetrical design of façades
Azay-le-Rideau - Blois (François I Wing overlooking courtyard, Loggia Façade overlooking the town) - Chambord (rear with its succession of windows) - Cheverny - Le Lude (inner façade) - Mongeoffroy - Serrant - Valençay - Villandry - Villesavin

Outstanding dormer windows
Amboise (Charles VIII Wing) - Azay-le-Rideau - Blois - Chambord - La Ferté-Saint-Aubin - Ussé - Villesavin
Classical and neo-Classical Architecture
Blois (Gaston d'Orléans Wing) - Cheverny - La Ferté-Saint-Aubin - Le Lude (overlooking courtyard) - Montgeoffroy - Serrant - Valençay

Chapels
Angers (St. Genevieve's) - Ambroise (St. Hubert's) - Chambord (Chapel Royal) - Le Plessis-Bourré - Loches (New apartments: Anne of Brittany's Chapel) - Meung-sur-Loire (12th-century underground chapel) - Montgeoffroy - Serrant - Ussé (collegiate church)

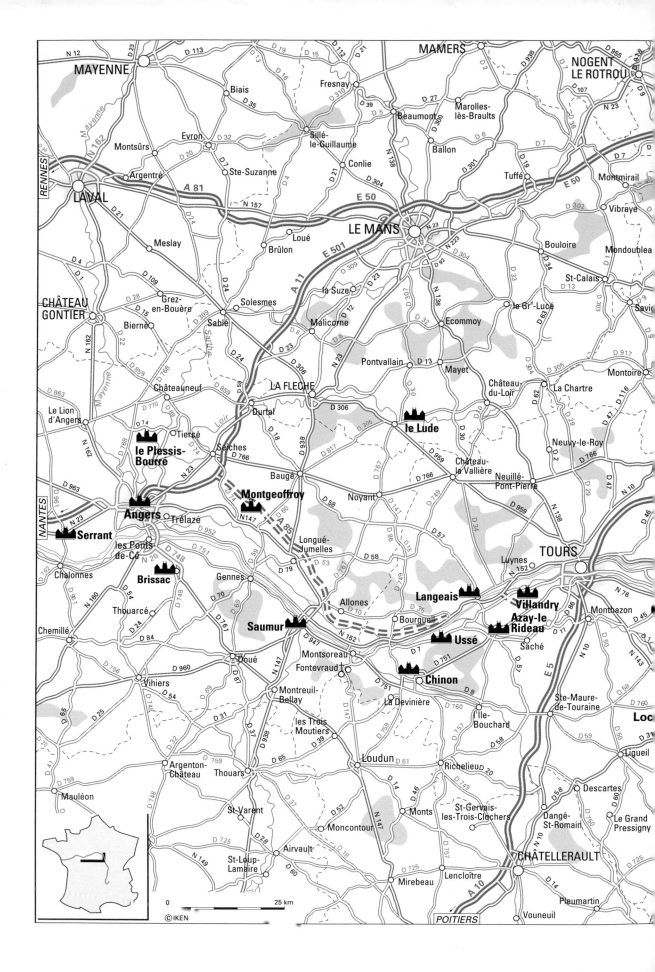

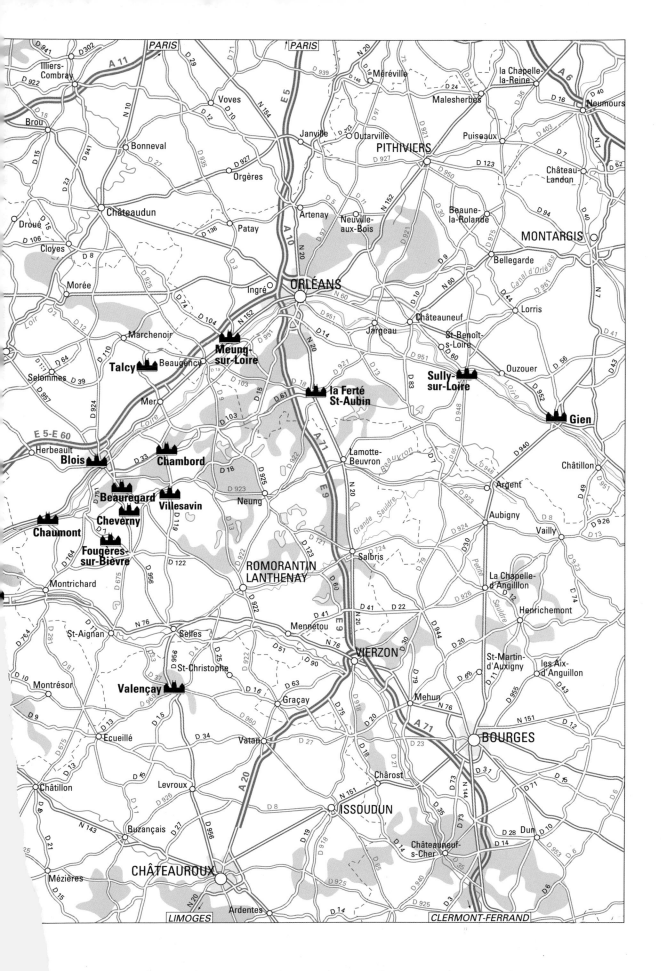

PHOTOGRAPHIC CREDIT

Our grateful thanks to the owners of Brissac who lent photographs free of charge.

Front cover: *Chambord*.
Back cover: *Sully-sur-Loire*.

© 1996 - Édilarge SA Éditions Ouest-France, Rennes
Cet ouvrage a été imprimé par Mame Imprimeurs à Tours (37)
I.S.B.N. : 2.7373.1966.8 - Dépôt légal : avril : 1996 - N° d'éditeur : 3355.02.06.01.97